GET YOUR

SHIT

TOGETHER

HOW TO GO FROM FEAR TO FREEDOM

AMY JOY

Testimonials

"Every once in a while, you meet someone whose life story is so moving, you just can't wait to see how many millions of people will benefit from learning the lessons she's learned from her remarkable journey. Sure enough, Amy Joy's book does just that. She has generously provided us with the inspiring fruits of her extraordinary commitment to heal, evolve, cut through the crap, and generously serve everyone she meets. Amy Joy – and her incredibly accessible book – is the real deal. For anyone wanting to learn how to turn lemons into the best lemonade you've ever tasted, this book will satisfy and nourish you in powerful and pragmatic ways."

Gary Malkin,
Emmy Award Winning Composer,
Public Speaker and Founder of *WisdomoftheWorld.com*

"On top of this book, Amy Joy's capacity to sense what's in the way of expressing your best self – and her ability to energetically remove and heal that which is in the way – is astonishing. Her book is a must-have for anyone interested in stepping up their game and going for the life of their dreams!

"Amy Is a master teacher, healer, and coach. Apply the principles she teaches in this book, and you will succeed, and avoid failure."

Rodolfo "Rudy" Rodriguez
CEO, Wingman Coaching LLC

"Reading this book has the potential of greatly improving your life in many ways. The lessons come directly from the author's personal experiences, and they are laid out in a simple but profound way. This book will teleport you right to the places where the amazing adventures took place, and you will personally experience the pain, the struggle, and the beautiful outcome that come from the victories of each situation."

David Mansilla
Founder & CEO, ISU Corp *www.isucorp.ca*
High-Tech Entrepreneur, International Best-selling Author

"Get Your Shit Together is a powerful reminder that life doesn't have to be perfect to be beautiful. In this book, Amy Joy shares relatable experiences that will make you laugh and cry, and most of all remind you that you are not alone. We all have shit! She also shares tangible tips and tools to shift your perspective and empower you to create a beautiful life, even when things don't turn out the way you hoped. Thank you, Amy, for sharing your heart and your brilliance with us."

Allison Maya Rose Rogers
Co-Founder of Legendary

"As a personal improvement and human performance specialist and having worked with thousands of people over the past 23 years, I find it rare to come across someone like Amy. Knowing her background and how much she walks her talk, having experienced her energy work, healing, and coaching, and now reading her book, I am floored by her resilience, compassion, generosity, and wisdom in every facet of life. I highly recommend anyone considering reading this book to stop hesitating and DO IT. Your greatnes is just on the other side of your confusion and fear, and Amy is a wonderful guide past your limits."

Nate Zeleznick
President & Co-founder of Vibravision®

"Read this book now because it will change your life!

Amy Joy leads you through the challenges she faced as a wife, mother, missionary and outcast from her religious community.

Her incredible journey of self discovery and healing will move you and equip you with breakthrough new tools and strategies to overcome any challenges you face in your life today.

– Christian Mickelsen,
#1 Best-Selling Author of "Abundance Unleashed"

Get Your Shit Together
How To Go From Fear To Freedom

All Rights Reserved

ISBN:
Paperback - 9781954759466
Hardcover - 9781954759473
EBook - 9781954759459

Cranberry Press Publish

My magical sons Brayden and Tate:
Being your mom has been my highest joy!
Thank you for being my teachers.
I love you!

To my amazing parents, Bill and Sheila, and my siblings, Karri and Jeremy:
You have stuck with me and loved me through thick and thin
— we are the best team!
I love you!

To Zander and Josh:
My life is exponentially better with you in it!
I love you!

My Love:
Thank you for being my rock,
my encourager, my safe place to fall.
I love you!

To Michael Drew and his wonderful team:
Together we made this book happen!
Thank you!

To all who encouraged me to fly towards my dreams:
Let's *SOAR!*

Table Of Contents

Introduction

Welcome to this exploration of breaking free of your self-imposed limitations!

Here you'll find how my story can help you change yours.

My name is Amy Joy.

I am currently a life coach (an intuitive breakthrough strategist), an energy healer, and I own a wellness center in Mexico. I chose these professions and created this center after years of searching to find my own truths and to free myself of the emotional and psychological baggage I carried with me for so long. I have benefited from years of private and group coaching, from spiritual journeys, and from personal counseling. In participating in all of these, I saw that I, too, could provide the tools to help others move ahead on their own journeys toward happiness and fulfillment.

I've had a full life. It's been wonderful and amazing and also filled with what some might call unfortunate incidents. I was raised in a religious community in Canada, one that put a strong emphasis on literal and often wrongheaded interpretations of the Bible, especially concerning the role of women. I spent years as a missionary myself, traveling and living in the jungle as far as Papua New Guinea. I've been a salesperson, a personal coach, a teacher's aide to special needs children and more. I've survived an abusive marriage. I'm the single mother of wonderful sons. I do my best to give back to my community. And I am happy and free in my life.

I want you to be happy and free, too. This is a step by step on how to go from Fear to Freedom! Freedom from suffering, freedom from feeling helpless, etc., and instead, to create and experience.

My story is one of overcoming hardships and forging a path forward as an empowered woman, mother, entrepreneur, and leader.

Throughout this book, you'll discover how I met the various challenges I faced — and how you can meet them, too, using steps I have put together so that you can begin to see how you can overcome what has been holding you back. My Mission is to liberate you from suffering and lead you into a life of freedom and joy, to a life you love!

This is divided into twelve chapters, and each chapter is divided into three or four sections.

Toward the end of each section is a series of steps, with explanations on how to do them.

Each step takes anywhere from one to five minutes. They're not a huge commitment in time — but I do ask that you commit to doing them. I suggest completing a chapter a week. It's perfect for book clubs as well.

In order to do that, I'd like you to fully concentrate on each step along the way, by beginning with a breathing exercise where you breathe deeply for a few minutes, releasing an "ahh" sound and allowing yourself to become centered, as if you're about to meditate. In fact, I'd like you to approach each step with the same open-mindedness you would bring to meditation. I urge you to do this for all steps, and I say this up front, rather than repeat the instructions multiple times.

Here's what I know... If you actually go through the steps and implement the necessary changes, you WILL experience transformation. You will experience progress, and progress = happiness!

You will soon get into the rhythm of letting yourself discover how to move ahead in your life and experience the freedom you have always longed for.

Are you *ready?*

Let's dive in!

 If you'd like further support from me, please use this QR. Looking forward to hearing from you!

Chapter 1

LITTLE AND LACKING

I was foolish to think that I had no value, yet for years that's what I believed.

In this chapter, I'm going to explore how from my experience, you can move beyond your limiting beliefs. I will show you how your past may shape you, but that it doesn't have to define you.

I will share several stories from my life that illustrate these points, and then I will share with you steps that you can take to figure out your own limiting beliefs, how to annihilate them, and create new, empowering beliefs!

I grew up in a small town in Canada, with two amazing parents and two younger siblings, Karri and Jeremy. At the beginning, my life was pretty peachy. I remember loving my world, and being happy.

Things changed when we moved to Ontario, when I was 7½ years old. We began to live and work at a mission organization that trains missionaries to go overseas and work with indiginous tribal people. This organization had many cultish tendencies that blew up my world and made me realize that I wasn't "in Kansas anymore," at least from my little girl's perspective.

Believing the Lies

The main change was going from a world where I believed I was free and loved unconditionally, to one where I felt trapped and judged. This was a world of control and rules. There were lots of great things about my childhood there, but what I struggled the most with was that women didn't have the same value as men.

I was angry at God for years for making me a girl! I remember standing on a hill where we lived, just before my eighth birthday, looking down at a pond, and I made the conscious choice that I was going to show them that girls were valuable, that I could do anything a boy could do, and that I could do it better. I realize now that this landmark moment shaped many of my other decisions: Who I married, what I fought for, what I chose to do and not do etc.

In essence, I refused the feminine and embraced the masculine. I became one of the biggest tomboys around. I walked like a boy, talked like a boy, acted like a boy. Most people watching me play soccer or hockey had no idea that I was a girl. I embraced the masculine in a big way. Again, it all stemmed from the fact that I needed to prove myself valuable.

The mission had very strict rules on what men could do and what women could do. There were no women in leadership roles anywhere. Women could take care of the children, but men had the right to tell you what to do and how to behave, and women would have to obey. They justified this from the Bible, insisting that men were the head of the household and that women were supposed to submit to them. I had a problem with this from the very beginning.

And so I fought like hell for years — to be noticed, to be valued, to be seen, to prove myself.

I became a driven, capable, hardworking, competitive, stressed-out, and overwhelmed human being.

Eventually, my stressed-out personality affected my kids. I hate to admit it, but they grew up with a very stressed-out mom. My need for perfection and for almost everything to be done at a super-high level of proficiency added so much stress to our world. The cost was huge, as I missed out on what could have been many funny, free, gloriously triumphant moments. I constantly looked for what was wrong, instead of what was right.

Now that I have come to understand the impact that my belief in my value and my resulting behaviors had on my children, I've apologized to them over and over. My beliefs also affected other people around me. My energy bled onto them all — pushing, forcing, proving. I'm now 46 years old, and I've held this core belief and attitude for more than 30 years. Obviously, it has left its mark.

My belief and attitude about having to prove myself also created many amazing experiences. I pushed through being uncomfortable to get to the other side of whatever I was creating. I'm not a quitter. I'm resilient, a go-getter. I've taken on huge projects like being a missionary in the middle of one of the most primitive tribal groups on the planet, I've built our houses with my own hands, I've helped build multiple airstrips, and I have traveled the world. Beautiful things have also come to pass through my belief that I needed to prove myself.

But it's important to look at both sides.

Years later, a co-worker sat down by me and said, "Okay. You're making me crazy."

I was surprised. "What are you talking about, Alex?"

"I wish that you would see yourself the way the rest of us do," he said. "Your homework tonight is to go home, and get naked. You need to stand in front of the mirror and look at yourself and go through every body part, starting from your toes all the way up to the top of your head and back down, telling yourself that you're beautiful."

This freaked me out. Simply his saying the word naked made me uncomfortable, because in the world where I grew up, no one talked about being naked. Or sex. No one spoke about anything like that.

Nevertheless, I listened to him. I went home and I got naked. I told myself I was beautiful. It was so weird, and so uncomfortable, that I wanted to crawl out of my skin. But I kept going, and I did it day after day after day after day, for probably a week, before I wasn't squirming any longer.

Alex's "homework" started a massive change in how I viewed myself. It was the first step in not refusing the feminine, In valuing myself, and noticing my beauty and my humanity, the way that I naturally am.

Steps and Methods

Here are a few suggestions on how you can identify your limiting beliefs.

Here's how to begin:

First, look back on a time in your childhood where something happened that created a new belief system for you. You have to know where you are on a map to get where you want to go. I learned that there are times in life when something happens that causes us to change our thinking, and our changed thinking affects all our future choices.

Now, I mentioned earlier that each of these steps involves centering yourself to focus. I will offer the full instructions here, but please remember that they apply to just about every step you will read in this book.

Center yourself.

- Sit in a quiet place, breathe in three times deeply.

  It's important to find a place with little or no distractions. I tend to go to my zen bed in my office because I know that that is where I have the best chance of no interruptions or distractions.

- Sit in a comfortable position.

  I sit cross-legged if I know I won't be sitting longer than 30 minutes. If I think I'll be sitting longer, I'll sit in a comfortable chair.

  Keep a good posture, with shoulders back and a straight spine, to keep energies flowing freely. Breathe at least three times deeply. When I say deeply, I mean, breathe as if you are breathing into the bottom of your stomach, like you are pouring water in and it's filling from the bottom first. You should do this because that is where the oxygen is collected by small bits of lung tissue called alveoli.

  Breathe in deeply, hold for a few seconds, and then exhale making the sound "ahhhhh." You want your exhale to be longer than your inhale so you get rid of any stale air in your lungs. I usually do this a least three times, but you can do it more if you like.

Ask your Higher Self, Intuition, God, Universal Intelligence, "What individual event in my life happened, that from that moment on, I believed and thought something different?"

Ask yourself, "What was my belief before the change happened?" It's important to write your answers down so you can see them clearly in front of you. When you do, you will realize you didn't always have that belief, that it was created from one impactful event in time.

In realizing this, you can also understand that you can change what you believe consciously. This can help you understand why you have been making the choices you have been making. When I realized that I had been working my ass off to prove myself to the world because of a choice made at 7½ years old, something shifted in me. My awareness of that alone helped evaporate the need for me to continue to do that. I can now choose to be competitive or not. Before I felt that, I didn't have a choice — I had to win, to be the best, to prove, prove, prove.

Ask yourself "What is my new empowering belief?" I now know that I am valuable because I exist. Period. It's important to replace the old bullshit belief with your new empowering one.

By following and implementing these steps, you will begin to understand that beliefs created in your past have a cost and consequences, but when you create a new, empowering belief that makes you feel great about yourself, this new belief will end up changing your life for the better. You have learned steps to enable you to do that:

- Look back on a time in your childhood where something happened that created a new belief system within you.

- Ask how it affected your life, and what the gifts and consequences of that belief were.

- What is your new empowering belief, now that you know you had a bullshit one?

You will learn how to appreciate the good that comes from that new belief, and in that, your past can heal the future!

Isn't Middle School a Bitch?

Is it possible to be unapologetically you?

We're exploring that here.

I'll share a story from my childhood that caused me to live many years of my life as a people-pleaser. Then I'll let you know what I did to turn that ship around. I'll provide you with some steps that you can take to find and accept yourself, so that you can live and be unapologetically you!

I grew up as a people-pleaser. Every day I worried about how to make everyone around me feel okay. This was what was expected in my environment, in the Mission Organization.

Our culture demanded that we be people-pleasers. There was an intense need to make sure that God was smiling on us, and the Mission leaders believed it was their job to make sure that we were always doing what we were supposed to be doing. If not, we were cast out or "asked to leave."

Once, when I was 13, I got the most beautiful dress that I had ever seen. You have to understand that I had fought with my mother almost every morning, for most of my life (or at least it feels like that), about wearing a dress to school. In my denial of the feminine, I played the role of being the tomboy. But I was also made fun of for being a tomboy.

My mom wanted me to be a girl, to look like a girl, to act like a girl. I didn't want any part of it. So almost every morning we fought over what to wear. There were very defined roles and rules: *Thou shalt listen, Thou shalt obey, Thou shalt look like a girl.* (To this day, the word *obey* gives me a little shiver.) In any event, I got this beautiful dress, and for the first time in my life that I could remember, I was actually enticed to wear it, thinking it looked pretty on me and that I was pretty in it.

I braved wearing this dress for our Tuesday night meeting, when we would gather like in a church service, and a man — always a man — would share something from the Bible. We all had to get dressed up to attend.

I walked in wearing my dress, and everyone stopped and stared at me. People weren't happy that I'd embraced my feminine side. They were uncomfortable and therefore made a big deal that I'd broken out of the role I'd assumed. That moment was traumatic for me as a new, fresh teenager. That was a moment that literally shaped a big part of the rest of my life.

I carried on being a tomboy for years, to the point where, when I got married, someone came up to me and said, "I thought you were going to walk down the aisle in sweatpants." I couldn't even wear a dress on my wedding day without causing a comment.

I felt that, having created the tomboy, I needed to wear it like a badge. I was a tough person. And yet I was dishonoring my feminine nature because it didn't feel safe to venture into it because it didn't feel safe, and because it made everybody uncomfortable. So I continued a life of people-pleasing as a tomboy who has to constantly prove herself.

The issue with people-pleasing is that you end up not living your own life.

You end up living somebody else's idea of what your life should be. I now see how this need to people-please stunted my growth. Stunted me becoming me. That had to change.

Steps and Methods

Here are the questions I asked myself to turn things around. You can too.

First, ask yourself: "What do I do to people-please?" What's important here is to know and understand when you are not being authentic and when you are pleasing people, so that you can create the opportunity to do things differently.

Ask yourself: "With whom was I, and am I, a people-pleaser?" and "Who am I afraid of?" and "In what situations have I been afraid to be myself?"

Ask yourself, "What has it cost me, being a people-pleaser?" Get real with yourself. Don't hide. Pretending cost me years of joy. What has it cost you?

Ask yourself, "What have I lost or not experienced because of my people-pleasing?" You know, actually, it's been shown that we will do more to avoid pain than to move toward pleasure. We need to feel the pain in order to want to make a change and move towards pleasure, so go deep with this question.

Ask yourself, "Where in my life have I not been authentic?" and "With whom have I not been authentic?" Sometimes these things are hard to face. But to do so is to become free. I wasn't authentic in many ways. At church. In my marriage. I was afraid to be me. I believed there was no room for me, only the men counted.

Write down at least three examples of when you are not authentic.

Finally, ask yourself, "Why is it important to be authentic?"

You have to understand why you want to make the change to living authentically, or else you never will. So why live authentically? Why make the change? What will you get out of living authentically? I now love being my unapologetic self. I know and accept that we are all different, and different is awesome. Write down at least three examples for each question.

The outcome is getting real clarity on how you have lived inauthentically so you can decide if you want to make a change.

Take action, but first know where you are and where you're going. For years, I simply went through the motions — until I realized I could change.

At the crossroads of choice, choose you. Just waking up to that is a huge step, and you should be proud of yourself for facing yourself. *Be you.* For many years I wasn't myself, and I paid the price. Don't let another moment pass you by as being someone other than the real *you*.

So how can you actually be *you*? How can you pull that off, after pretending for so long? You do it one step at a time. One little choice at a time. For me, this meant saying no. I needed to say no to my marriage, no to the control of the Mission, no to the idea that I must stay single for the rest of my life because the Bible says so. *No.*

The outcome of these steps is true change for you. Step by step, over and over, you will build the muscle of not giving a care about what others think. And practice makes perfect.

By following and implementing these steps, you will learn how to have a very clear idea of how and where and whom you try to please. You will gain real clarity as to how you have lived inauthentically so that you can decide if you want to keep living that way or make a change. You will do this by asking these questions:

- What do you do to *people-please*?

- What have you lost or not experienced because of your *people-pleasing*?

- Why be the opposite of that — why be the real, authentic *you*?

Step by step, over and over, do you, *be yourself*, no matter what.

Step by step, you will build the muscle of not giving a flying flip about what others think. You will know that being yourself is more valuable than pretending to be what someone else wants you to be.

Small — but Mighty!

Sometimes you have to lead by example. Here, I'm exploring those times when you have to lead by example and help others live their authentic selves.

I will share a story about a mission trip to Panama, and then share with you steps to become a leader by standing up for your truth.

When I was 17, I flew to Panama for my first Mission trip. It was an amazing experience. I had raised the money to go through the help of supporters and friends, and I even had enough money left over to enable a friend to accompany me.

In the first four weeks of the mission, we built a school in a little town called Chame, where the Mission base was located. We also repaired an airstrip in the middle of the jungle near the Darién region, on the border of Panama and Colombia. We worked about eight hours a day as a group, and we accomplished quite a lot.

One night, it was time for our team meeting, and John — one of the missionaries from the tribal village where we were headed next — stopped by to brief us on what to expect, and to lay out the plans for the coming days. It was announced that the boys would be hiking into the tribe, and that the girls and any boys who didn't want to hike would be flying in. My head snapped back as I thought, 'Hell no! No way I'm missing out on the experience of a lifetime!' So I spoke up and expressed my desire, leaving out the word hell, of course. The team leaders flatly told me that no girls were allowed to hike in.

I was determined. There was no way that I was going to miss out on this experience. So I continued to insist. And they kept telling me, "No." The team leaders ended up asking me to come into a separate room. One of them said, "Amy, you need to stop this. You can't go. It's not good for you to go. It's only for the boys." I responded with my favorite question: "Why?" My team leaders were actually from my Mission back in Canada. They knew me. They grew up with me; they knew I was a badass. They knew that I played sports with the boys; they knew who I was. So I asked, "You know me! What is going on here?"

They were under pressure, like everyone at the Mission. They feared what people would think if word got out that they had let girls hike to the jungle village. But they also knew that I was quite capable of doing it. So I just kept pushing, and, finally, I got John the missionary on my side. And like music to my ears, I heard him say, "It's okay. If she feels she can do it." He looked at me and said, "She can come." At that moment, my soul screamed, "Yes!"

As a result, other girls there were inspired to hike with me. But they were too scared to speak up. So I went and faced the leadership again and said, "If I'm going, so will they." Again, it was another big hubbub: "No, no, no, they can't do it!" I insisted, "Yes, they can." And, long story short, we all got to go!

So I had this amazing experience because I stuck to my guns and because I refused to back down.

Honestly, I was scared. It was not easy to face the leadership in my world. It was their way always. You could get kicked out. You were either in trouble because God wasn't smiling on you, or you were rebellious, or you were a backslider. You'd be labeled with one of those terms, which could then affect people's opinion, not only of you, but also of your parents, who were also part of the Mission. This, then, was a big moment for me.

All the same, I had an epic experience. The boys and a few girls and I took a battered bus down the Pan American highway, all the way to the end of the road. Literally. The bus had to do a 10-point turn to get turned around. We got out after a five- or seven-hour drive.

We had chickens and tons of people in the bus, and everyone was standing in the aisles. It was packed and hot. When we got to the end of the road, we started hiking. It started pouring torrential rain, forcing us to slog through the mud.

Over the course of several hours, we hiked through the jungle to a humble cabin with a couple of little buildings surrounding a house for the chickens and other animals. We were greeted by beautiful, kind people. We'd arrived at dark, and they killed and cooked a couple of chickens for our dinner.

The four of us girls slept sideways in a double bed. Rats and other rodents scurried around. It was my first introduction to cockroaches. It was a little freaky.

Awakening in the morning, we realized we were covered in mud. We hadn't seen ourselves clearly before. But after cleaning up a bit, we started hiking again, and we set off for the river. Again, it started raining, and for hours and hours we hiked and hiked and hiked. We girls leaned on each other, and made sure that we all got safely to the river.

At the river, we found tribal people with their dugout canoes. A dugout canoe is literally a tree that's dug out, so you can sit in it and float. And they tend to tip over. The tribal people helped us into their boats. I remember lying in two inches of water against a big stalk of bananas. I had never seen a stalk of bananas. I didn't know that bananas came on a massive stalk. There must have been 100 bananas on it!

The tribal people used poles to steer their boats, with one person in the front, and the other in the back. It seemed that almost every time they pushed off, more water would come in over the top. But I was in heaven. I was so happy to be on that adventure. I love adventure. I was sitting there with a huge smile on my face, when I suddenly felt a sting on my shoulder. Looking down, I saw the largest ant I'd ever laid eyes on! Its pincers were enormous. I grabbed it with my shirt and yanked it out of my skin. It made a big welt, and I thought, 'Oh, wow! Here we go!'

There were literally boa constrictors hanging from the trees, and alligators resting on the riverbanks. I thought I was in a jungle adventure movie. To this day, it was the most epic river trip I've ever been on. I couldn't have been happier. I couldn't have been in a more blissful state than I was on that adventure. Had I not fought for it, had I not insisted, I would never have had that incredible adventure. I would never have had that experience. I would have settled for something a lot less (getting flown in, not hiking in) and not had that adventurous story to tell.

Steps and Methods

Here's how you can learn from my experience:

Step 1. Become aware of what you really want.

What's important about this step is that sometimes, without noticing, we live our lives for others instead of for ourselves.

So, when you hear something that doesn't sound quite right to you, such as, "You can't go because you're a girl," you don't have to accept that. Pay attention to how you feel. Emotions affect our physical bodies, and the more we pay attention to our bodies and emotions, the more we can consciously decide what to do next. The best way to do this is to stop and listen to your inner voice and scan your body with your intention. This can take only a few seconds, but it's important to do it.

Ideally, after contemplating you realize that if it seems like bullshit to you, then call it bullshit. Don't settle. When you label it like that, it can help you separate it out from the program. So many of us have been programmed to just take whatever is thrown at us. If it seems like bullshit to you, call it as it is — bullshit! I usually say this out loud, which makes it more real for me. You can say it internally, too, if you want, but acknowledging it out loud is the key.

This step is all about getting the full understanding of what it is that you really want in life.

Step 2. Decide if it's worth going for, or not — know why you want to fight to have it.

First center yourself and breathe. Ask your higher self, the universal intelligence in you and all around you, for clarity.

Ask yourself, "What are the consequences if I don't go for it?" This is about picking your battles. Pick only the ones that are the most important to you, or else you could be fighting all the time.

Ask yourself, "If I don't stand up, then what's the benefit?" If it turns out that this is worth fighting for, then take some extra time to get even more clear. The benefit for me was wanting and then having that experience. So ask yourself and then write down a list of benefits and reasons to make a stand.

Ask yourself, "What is the cost?" Reflect on this, and write down your answers. For me, the cost was missing out on an epic adventure just because someone else wanted me to, without a solid, truly justifiable reason.

Ask yourself, "Is it worth it?" Then make your choice. Fear could rear its ugly head at such a moment as this. Ask the question again. Your intuition will tell you what you feel. At that moment, make your choice of what you really want to do. Josh, my coach, teacher, guru, and healer, taught me this. "If you seek an answer and don't find it, then that's your answer." Wait. You might need to wait for the right time.

This step helps you have clarity and understanding of the cost and consequence for fighting or not fighting for what you really want.

Stand up, speak up, insist, add value, be persistent — lead.

What's important is that if the cost is too great, and you don't choose to go with what is right for you, then you will resent yourself and the people involved, not knowing what might have happened if you had tried.

Know what you really want to do. This is the first step. Take the time to listen to your higher self. Clarity and conviction will bring you faster to your desired outcomes.

Speak up and express yourself. Push through the fear.

I used to be terrified, because in the world I grew up in, you didn't question authority. I needed to start saying what I thought and needed. The importance of expressing yourself is massive. You don't need anyone else's permission to want what you want, to like what and who you like. It is important to express yourself! So let it out!

The outcome of this step is to express yourself in a mature, controlled way with strength and conviction to get *your* desired outcome.

Ask yourself, "Who followed me, and how did that impact their lives?" Understand that your choices often affect others.

Minimize damages. Take responsibility. In my case during that Panama trip, I did all I needed to do, with no complaint, and I helped and contributed where I could.

Make it a win-win for everyone. I also was able to help and encourage the other girls that they could do it, which empowered them, and they created a new standard for themselves on what they could do and what is possible for them.

You have the ability to impact the lives of others and to make clear that what you want is what others may also want. By leading the charge, you can enlist others and everyone gets what they want.

Sometimes, you need to lead by example. Sometimes, you need to step up and fight the current system. It is important to be sure about what's important to you, so when the time is right, you can stand up and speak your truth. Again, do this by asking these questions or following these steps:

- Become clearly aware of whatever it is that you really want.

- Decide if it's worth going for or not; know why you want to fight to have it, and what the consequences are if you don't go for it.

- Stand up, speak up, insist, add value, be persistent — lead.

This allows you to stay congruent with yourself, to experience things that your heart desires, and to inspire others to do the same.

Being in alignment with yourself is important. Taking risks is the only way out of the bog, but it's worth it!

Now, I'd like you to reflect once more on where you are, why you do what you do, and how you can continue to grow. I know I've spoken a lot about my past and my adventures. But, really, I do that to give you examples of real-world experience. In the end, this is all about you.

Next, we will explore relationships, how I navigated them, and how you can learn from my failures and successes.

 If you'd like further support from me, please use this QR. Looking forward to hearing from you!

Chapter 2

LOVE, MARRIAGE, TRUST, AND PERSPECTIVE

Life doesn't fit into the perfect little box you think it does. I woke up to this the hard way, through a disastrous, abusive marriage. I explore that here, as well as my years of emotional subjugation, and my decision to build a life for myself and my children on my own.

I will share with you the steps you can take to become aware of your reality and what to do to change it. You will learn how to define where you have been blind to your reality and how you can choose what you want. You will also have the ability to take inventory of all your blessings.

Six months after our marriage, I knew for sure that life was very different than what I'd envisioned. The man I married wasn't the man I thought he was. Overnight, he became a monster.

Things completely changed on our wedding day. That very day he started being an asshole. While we dated, everything was great, and I thought I knew him. I didn't expect him to be otherwise than how he seemed during our dating. I later realized that he had played the part of a loving boyfriend until the moment he had me. He knew that in our Mission culture, he had power over me in marriage. As soon as he married me, the true person emerged. For his sake, I won't use his name. Let's just call him Joe (apologies to all the good Joes out there).

A Hard Reality

It was a hard reality. I was in denial about it for years. I kept believing Joe would see the way. That his anger, the emotional, psychological, and sexual abuse would end. But they didn't. Everything got worse.

Before we traveled to Papua New Guinea to be missionaries there, I even said to him, "We have no right to go. We are living a false existence in front of our churches and our supporters." As a missionary, friends, family, and supporting churches send you money. They support you in your work. I felt hugely responsible to our supporters, and I felt that we were living a lie.

I begged him multiple times for counselling, to get help, but he refused. So when I threatened not to go to Papua New Guinea, he went back to acting like the person I dated and the person I thought I was marrying. This lasted a few months. By the time we got to Papua New Guinea, things were back to the abusive way they were before. At that point, I was pregnant, with all the related morning sickness and such, and married to a man who didn't give a shit about me or our baby. After our first two weeks in Papua New Guinea, I started bleeding. I had placenta previa, which is potentially fatal.

A Mission nurse put me on bed rest. For two weeks, I laid in bed, scared out of my mind that I was losing my baby. Meanwhile, Joe was off doing his own thing. I was a massive inconvenience to him. I would lie in bed all day in 100 degree heat. When he returned, I'd ask him nicely if he could get me something to eat. He would get angry, stomp off, come back and throw a piece of toast my way.

This was how I started my life in Papua New Guinea. The nurse told me I had to go back to Canada to have the baby for health reasons. Joe didn't want to do that, but for the sake of what everyone would think, he begrudgingly flew back to Canada with me. He made me pay every day for the fact that I and the baby were inconveniencing him in his dream of being in New Guinea. I learned how to appease, to stay out of the way, to make sure the food was ready, to give him sex whenever he wanted it — just to appease the monster in him.

Our baby, Brayden, was a beautiful miracle. Two months after I gave birth, we flew back to Papua New Guinea. I felt like I was stuck on the same train of life and couldn't get off. I was barely making it every day. Trying to keep Brayden safe, trying to keep him out of his father's way. Trying to avoid conflict.

I didn't know whom to go to for help. No one would believe me. People I spoke with downplayed my situation or talked to Joe on my behalf, which made him worse. I felt completely alone in the middle of the jungle, surrounded by tribal people, with the stress of the medical work, people dying, and people needing me and, by the way, I was not trained for any of this. I was delivering babies and stitching people up and pulling arrows out of people's legs and trying to save them from malaria, pneumonia, and whooping cough, and then on top of all that, coming home to that situation, to that darkness. It was really, really tough. Two years later, Tate was born. And I remember feeling really guilty for bringing another child into this mess of a home. And yet, I was so thankful to have a purpose, and to have a distraction from my reality.

My existence was to serve him. I was there for whatever Joe needed. My saving grace was being able to watch Oprah, thanks to a satellite dish that allowed us to receive TV from Indonesia. The kids would go down for their naps, and I would watch an hour of Oprah every afternoon and disappear into a happy place. It was from watching those shows, and seeing and hearing the stories of people and women getting empowered that I realized that this is NOT okay and that I don't have to settle for it.

I knew that I had to stop doing what everyone else was telling me to do, and I needed to fight for myself and my voice. Something had to change. I didn't know how I could leave, but I knew that I couldn't let anybody know, because he'd kill me. I couldn't embarrass him. I couldn't humiliate him in any way.

We were due for furlough (a year off to visit family and supporting churches). I knew that if I was to run, it would have to be then. As we packed to go home, in my gut, in my intuition, I knew that this was probably it, that this was going to be the end, that I might not be coming back to the place where I had intended to be for the next 15 to 20 years. That my life as a missionary was over. You're not allowed to be a missionary if you're divorced in this Mission. With tears running down my cheeks, I packed up, knowing deep down that I might never be back. I looked at the faces of my Mission partners whom I loved, and the tribal people to whom I had given my life for the past few years and grieved. I loved them and I missed them all already, especially Madagumbe, my best girlfriend in the village.

I was still not completely sure what I was going to do, so we got on the plane and we flew back. I remember the lights of Los Angeles. I'll never forget. It was the first time in years that I'd seen America. I saw the lights of L.A. and I prayed to God, and I said, "Lord, help me. Show me what to do." I made a choice that I was going to go. I didn't know when, and I didn't know how. But at that moment, I knew that I would. I had to for the sake of the boys, for the sake of myself. In those days that followed, when I realized that my dream of a loving husband and father in Joe was an impossibility, I should have cried. I should have wailed and screamed. I should have let the grief out. But I didn't. I kept most of it in, in part because I was afraid Joe would figure out what I was doing, but also because I thought I would be "less than" if I cried or got angry. I know now that that is not healthy, but that was how I was in those days.

Without going into too much detail, but to give you an idea of what it was like living with Joe, I'm actually copying this down from a document that I wrote years later right after this incident took place.

I was driving Brayden to school when he was 6 years old, and he asked if he could talk to me about something about dad. I said sure. He said "Why did dad spank us so hard?" I said, "Oh, I know, honey. Daddy was so angry, so much, that he would do that. That's why mommy took you and Tate away. I used to talk to dad and ask him not to spank, to be nice, to be gentle, but daddy didn't change. That's why I took you to a safe place."

Brayden said, "Yeah. And I remember when daddy chased you down the hall and you went into the bathroom. Why, mom?"

I said, "Well, because mommy was scared of daddy and what he might do. And the bathroom was the only room in the house that I could lock myself in."

Brayden looked up at me and said something I'll never forget for as long as I live. He said, "I should have gotten a lock for my room." At that moment, my heart literally split in half, and it seemed that all the memories from those days came flooding back. All the rage, violence, and fear that we lived with. The feelings of guilt that I should have left sooner, and the feelings of relief that at least I left when I did. All of it all at once flooded my mind and heart.

And I said, "Oh honey, I know. That's why we left. That's why I can't be married to daddy. No little boy or wife should be afraid of their dad or husband. No boys should be afraid in their own house."

I am so thankful that once I left, I stayed gone.

Steps and Methods

Here are some suggestions for how you can become aware of what you are settling for:

Center yourself and breathe. Ask your higher self for clarity.

Become aware of the reality of the death of a dream. Becoming aware is really the first and most important step.

Ask yourself, "Where in my life have I been an ostrich refusing to truly see what is going on?" It's difficult at times to face yourself like this, but when you do, you can create the change you actually need. Keep breathing deeply throughout this exercise.

Define that death of a dream. For me, discovering that my dream of a happy healthy marriage and home was actually dead was one of the hardest things I've ever had to face.

Decide if you are staying or leaving the situation. Make a conscious choice to either stay and accept what is, or leave and change the situation.

Ask yourself, "What are the pros and cons if I stay?" and, "What are the pros and cons if I change the situation?" Listen to your inner voice, without judgment or analysis. Ask yourself the above question again and again until you run out of ideas and you have a good list.

With a situation this big, get some outside help from someone you trust. Outside perspective can really help, as sometimes we can't see past our own blinders. Once you have sought counsel and made your choice, it's important that you decide ahead of time that you will go all in with whatever choice you make.

Ask yourself, "What lessons have I learned? What gifts have I received?" Look back and discover what gifts came from the situation regardless of how difficult it was. I do this step by sharing that I learned how strong I really am and how there's nothing God and I can't handle.

Ask yourself, "What good has come from this situation?" If you don't ask and answer this, you will be likely pulled into the common program of being a victim.

Ask yourself, "What have I learned, specifically, that I maybe wouldn't have if this didn't happen?" Write down anything that comes to mind. Rejoice in those things. Allow yourself to feel good about that. I learned what love isn't — which is invaluable! Make your list of specific things that you learned.

Ask yourself, "Who else has benefitted from this situation?" Write down anything that comes to mind. Smile, rejoice in those things. Allow yourself to feel good about that. Take inventory of all the blessings that have taken place because of the situation. This new perspective of gratitude turns the trauma into a blessing.

By following and implementing these steps, you will learn how to deal with the death of dreams and turn them into gifts . You will learn how to define where you have been blind to a death of a dream, and to allow the emotions out to appropriately grieve it. You will also know how to consciously and non reactively choose what you want for your life. You will have the steps to take to rebuild, and choose a new way for your life:

- Become aware of the reality of the death of a dream.

- Decide if you are staying or leaving the situation.

- What lessons were learned, what gifts received.

- Turn fear into freedom, and trauma into triumph.

Get Me Out of This Cage!

Have you ever felt completely and utterly trapped?

Here, I will share the story of my escape from my abusive marriage. I will also provide you with some steps that can help you move ahead when you feel stuck and in need of a change. You will learn how to make wise, conscious choices for yourself without negatively affecting people around you.

I wasn't just leaving an abusive husband. I was leaving everything that I knew and loved and was part of. It was definitely one of the biggest decisions of my life.

For the sake of the kids, there was no other way. Once we reached Los Angeles from Papua New Guinea, we visited churches and friends in Montana. From there we traveled to Pennsylvania, my ex-husband's home state. His parents were there, the in-laws from hell, especially his mother. One evening I came to bed after Joe, I asked him nicely to move over, since I was seven-and-a-half months pregnant and was as big as a barn.

He reacted with violence. He sat up with a roar and whipped me repeatedly with the bed sheets. I curled up in a ball and covered my belly with my hands to try to protect our unborn son, Tate.

As fast as the abuse started, it ended, and he lay down and went right back to sleep. Needless to say, I did not. I lay there shaking, scared, and overwhelmed with the idea that I was bringing life into this mess, again. The next morning I got brave and told his mom what happened, hoping from one mom to another that she would finally see and help me. She listened to me, and quickly got up and started making breakfast without a word. It was never spoken about again.

During our time in Pennsylvania, my parents and my sister visited from Canada and Michigan to see me. It was breaking-point time. One evening, I went out into the hallway and my dad was there. I leaned over and whispered into his ear, "As soon as we have the chance, we're running."

I had finally made the decision that now was the time to escape. It was such a relief simply to have made the decision. We went for breakfast to see a friend and we planned for my dad to stay back so that he could call the Pastor, because, if I was going to leave, I wanted to do it with the blessing of the church. I also wanted a witness that wasn't family, that I wasn't just acting randomly, blindly, or emotionally. This was real. This was needed. Once the Pastor knew the full situation, he told my dad to get me and the kids to a safe place ASAP.

So we came back from breakfast. Joe was in his normal angry and ornery mood. He said he was going to head to his parents and work in the basement. The tension went through the roof. We decided to take the kids to McDonald's, hoping that he would leave while we were away.

When we thought we were gone long enough for Joe to leave, we drove back to the house. We pulled into the garage, and we burst into action. We each took a floor. My sister took the kids into the basement and with them got the toys. My mom took the main floor, I took the upstairs, and my dad stood at the door of the garage and loaded the van. We would throw our clothes in garbage bags, and he would take them and load the van. We were very careful to take only what belonged to me or the boys. As soon as that van was full, my dad lifted the garage door, parked that one on the street, and moved the other van in to load that one up.

I sat at the kitchen table and wrote Joe a letter, explaining exactly what I was doing and why I was doing it. That I had the blessing of the Pastor. That my family had left to go back home, and that I was somewhere safe. I needed him to think I wasn't with my family, in order to keep them safe and buy us some time to get away! I was very clear in the letter that he needed to get professional help.

We tore off, and we were only thirty minutes down the road when my phone started blowing up from him with ring after ring. We had arranged for the Pastor to wait there at the house for Joe when he came back. Pastor Scott later said to us that what he witnessed in Joe at that time he couldn't believe or unsee. He was so relieved to know we were safe.

I didn't answer my phone, and we hotel-hopped for a few days so that he couldn't find us. It was so incredibly stressful. I felt all emotions all at once. I felt relieved and guilty, happy and sad. Scared and more scared. I felt guilty because of the programming I'd had and the control that he had had on me for seven-and-a-half years. Psychologically, he was still in control of me. I was physically free, but not free yet emotionally or psychologically. I would learn that this takes years to heal.

The miracle was that we actually got away safely!

We ended up crossing the border into Canada, where mom and dad lived. We went straight to the police, and they told us what to do. I remember for the first time telling my story out loud in full to the lawyer.

It was the first time my dad had heard the full story as well. I could see the horror and sadness in his eyes as I spoke. I remember feeling validated, for the first time.

I was thankfully able to get full custody. It was at my absolute discretion whether or not the kids saw their father, which I later found out is super unusual. That was another miracle of God's protection over us.

Steps and Methods

You don't have to be in an abusive marriage to be stuck. Here are some things you can do to get unstuck.

Step 1. Be aware of being stuck. When you're stuck, you need to act.

Wake up. Become fully aware of your situation. Ask yourself, "How deep in the mud am I? How long have I felt trapped?" Awareness is almost always the first step!

Choose. Make a choice, stay or go. Accept what is or make a change. Jump in or jump out. When you feel a sense of relief or peace, you know that you are on the right track. You will probably still have fear, but as long as you feel that peace, that knowing, then that's your answer. The problem is we seldom take the time to ask. Keep seeking until you have the answer, and then go with it.

To recap: Wake up to your position and also make a conscious choice to do something about it.

Step 2. Get creative. Understand that you may have to be creative in order to get unstuck in the best possible way.

Ask yourself, "What's the best way to move into the new direction I need to go, with the least amount of damage to me and others?" Weigh the pros and cons. I figured out pretty quickly that leaving openly would probably have ended up with someone dead. I had to leave in secret. Walk yourself through it. The right course for you will become clear.

Create two or three plans of attack. We have our logical mind, and we also have our higher self, our intuition, some call it the Holy Spirit. Circle the parts of the plan that feel the best, and create a step-by-step process for each part.

Choose which one is plan A and which is plan B. My plan A took place. Plan B was that, if we got caught trying to leave and made it out alive, I would have called Pastor Scott and got him involved. Hopefully, your situation isn't a life-or-death one, but the process is the same. I've used this process many times for different challenges, and it works really well.

Step 3. Get Brave. Realize that it is going to take courage to get yourself out of the pickle you've got yourself into.

Take stock of where you are right now, acknowledge any fears. Write down everything that comes to mind. Then rewrite the list under a new category. One is, "Things I can control," and another is, "Things that are out of my control." It's a great way to sort out your thoughts.

Do the things you can do right now, one bit at a time. Tony Robbins, the popular self-help guru, says, "Progress equals happiness." So every step is progress, and that means you can choose to be happy about that progress. Write down your answers. In escaping from my marriage, the only way I actually accomplished that was by taking one step at a time.

Burn the boats. There's no going back. Often, when we come up against something that is new or that is hard, we turn around and run the other way from where we were headed. Making a conscious choice will help you not run back to something you know you need to change. This process helped me actually leave.

This step helps you know how to be brave, and how to get to the point emotionally where you can make the move to freedom.

Step 4. Move. Take massive action. Understand and accept that it will take a massive action to get unstuck.

Take the first step. Tell someone what you are going to do. Determine when the best time to take the first step is based on what you know. Set the time and date, and then do it. Then let someone know your plan so that you have accountability and help, if needed.

Get help if you can. If you are able to get help or support on your journey to change, do it! Just make sure they are actually helping and supporting. Be careful not to choose people who might resist your plan and direction or sabotage it. Thankfully I was able to escape with my parents' and my sister's support! I am so thankful that I had them. They were able to take care of the kids while I dealt with logistics and my own intense emotions.

Don't "do" life alone. We are not meant to be islands unto ourselves. Get some help, allow people to support you. Appreciate them while they do it. They are there to support you.

Take the next step. Ask yourself what your next "baby step" is, and do it. I remember when we crossed the U.S.-Canada border. With the guard shack in the rearview mirror, I realized I had done it. We were safe.

By following and implementing these steps, you will learn how to be aware, brave, and how to take the necessary action to reclaim your life. In the end, you will learn how to make wise, conscious choices for yourself with the least people negatively affected around you, and how to get to the point where you are emotionally able to make a move for freedom.

You will do that by asking these questions of yourself:

- How far in the mud am I? How long have I felt trapped?

- Do I want to stay stuck or trapped, or am I willing to do whatever it takes to experience freedom?

- What is my new conscious choice?

- What's the best way to move into the new direction I need to go, with the least amount of damage to me and others?

- What are the two best plans? Which one is plan A and which one is plan B?

- How am I feeling right now — What fears do I have?

- What can I do right now toward my goal — What is the next step?

Burn the boats. There's no going back.

Take the first step (tell someone what you are going to do).

Get help if you can.

Ask yourself over and over what your next baby step is, and do it.

Ultimately you will be able to pull yourself out of the mud and then out of the cage in order to live YOUR life.

It Is Easy to Dodge Our Responsibility

What's my responsibility in this? This is the question I asked myself as I looked at my situation of being in an abusive marriage.

We are all responsible for the lives we have created for ourselves. I repeat. We are all responsible for the lives we have created for ourselves. Here, you will learn the steps on how to figure out your responsibility in a situation, how to know who else has been affected by your choices and how to make it right, and how to take a new and inspired action. This will help you understand how your situation not only affects you, but everyone around you. By the end, you will have a new plan to move ahead.

Everybody in your life is a mirror of something that's also in you. Joe was such a bully, and I was appalled that I might be too. What we see in others exists in us in some way. During my marriage, as I asked myself how I got there, and what led me into an abusive relationship, the hardest question to face was this: "What's my responsibility in this?"

I realized I'd been a bully to my sister. I didn't respect her, and I treated her terribly. I physically beat up on her "playing around," because I was so tough and she wasn't. She was a very feminine girly-girl and loved to play dress-up and with dolls. I was the one with the hockey posters on the walls and soccer balls and trophies everywhere... We couldn't have been more different. Instead of embracing our differences, I scorned her.

I asked myself if the bullying in me attracted the bully Joe. Or was it that I didn't feel I had value? That I valued myself so little that I didn't think I could leave. I believe it was both. For years, I blamed the church and blamed the Mission for feeding my brain with the belief that once you were married, you were always married and there was no out. But the reality was at some point, I called bullshit and I did leave. So I could have left sooner.

When I left, I also took responsibility for what I did. And I later apologized to my sister for all the years of bullying her.

In taking responsibility, I also needed to apologize to my parents and to thank them profusely for all the support and all that they had done for me in all these years of running, protecting and helping me. I also apologized to my second husband, Pete, who was highly affected by my life and my situation. When we married, I wasn't ready to remarry. I was not yet healed. I did not understand my needs. I was not the best partner for Pete. I am truly sorry for the pain that I caused him. I am, however, thankful that he was in my life as well, because he was and is an amazing dad to my boys.

With this awareness I get to do things differently. I get to choose differently. Awareness is a beautiful thing.

But you can't do things differently unless you know what to change.

Steps and Methods

Here are some suggestions for how you can learn from me.

Step 1. Ask yourself, "What is my responsibility in this situation?" We are all responsible for the lives we have created for ourselves.

Ask yourself, "How did I get here?" You are responsible for your life. Period. The sooner you realize that the better. We have been taught to be victims, to blame everyone else for our shitty life. It's a lie, it's simply not true and deep down you know it too.

Ask yourself, "What did I have to believe about life, people, myself to tolerate this?" Write down anything that comes to mind, even if you don't like it or want to believe it. I believed life was hard and so I expected hard things to happen.

Ask yourself, "What did I do to contribute to this situation?" Write down anything that comes to mind. What do you have to discover about yourself? What have you done to contribute to your situation? By taking responsibility, we stop being a victim and we start taking care of our own shit.

Step 2. Ask yourself, "Who has been affected by my actions?" Then apologize to them.

It's important to look around and see the carnage you've left in your wake. Ask yourself, "Who else has been affected by me and my choices?" Write down anyone who comes to mind, without judgment.

Ask yourself, "How have I affected them specifically?" It's important that you dig deep and really contemplate how exactly you affected the people around you. For me, I had to take responsibility for staying so long with Joe and for what it did to my sons, Brayden and Tate. They were quite young, but they felt and understood a lot.

Apologize for your part in impacting others' lives in whatever way you did, and ask them, "What am I missing? How else did my choices affect you?"

Think deeply about this, and then contact everyone on the list and set up a time to talk to them privately. Then honor that time by showing up and apologizing to them.

Also ask them, "What am I missing — how else did my choices impact you?" You might not realize half of it. Let them speak freely. Do not interrupt them or get defensive. Listen and apologize, and take ownership for how your life and choices affected their life. It's amazing how healing this is and how much those people appreciate you taking the time to apologize and honor them in that way.

Thus, you can make things right and clean things up with the people in your life that you have impacted!

Step 3. Take new and inspired action. This step is important because in order to get a different result, you need to actually do things differently.

Ask, "If I don't want to be here, where do I want to be?" It's important to decide where you want to be — and who you want to be. Write down anything that comes to mind.

Ask, "Why do I want that specifically?" Write down anything that comes to mind. I needed to physically move so that I could live and feel safe.

Ask, "What do I need to do and who do I need to be to get that result?" Now it's time for action. Without action, things keep swirling around in our minds and nothing changes. When you know what you need to do, schedule it. Make an appointment, take the class, sign up for the course, or take the vacation. Do not delay another day.

By following these steps, you will learn how to take responsibility. You will do this by asking these questions:

- What is my responsibility in this situation?

- Who has been affected by my actions (so you can apologize to them)?

- What is my new inspired action step?

Life is messy — your energy, actions and attitudes affect others, and it's important to minimize the damages and also honor the people in your life that have stuck it out with you in the swamp.

Next we will look at how you can change your perspective, which will have a profound impact on your life.

 If you'd like further support from me, please use this QR. Looking forward to hearing from you!

Chapter 3

CHANGE YOUR PERSPECTIVE, CHANGE YOUR LIFE

What if everything you've ever gone through is worth it?
And I mean EVERYTHING.

Here I am going to share where exactly I was able to truly see and understand the phrase: Change your perspective, change your life.

We've all heard the phrase "Perspective is everything." It really is. How you see things determines how you feel about things, which determine your actions on what's going to happen next. When you change your perspective you change your life. You no longer act on programmed thoughts. You can separate yourself from that and you can say, "Wait a second. What is true? What else could be true?"

You will learn steps on how to look back on any trauma and ask yourself what good has come from it, among other questions. Learn how to embrace, share the energy of gratitude, and create a new reality.

The beautiful thing about changing your awareness is that you get to change your perspective. For years, I was a victim. I saw myself as a victim, even though to people looking at me, I seemed to have it all together. I realized this wasn't true. Tony Robbins teaches this, and it's my favorite phrase, "Life is happening *for* me, not *to* me."

Now I see this everywhere, because I've reprogrammed my mind and changed my perspective. I had such a glorious moment once with Brayden as we were driving home. I picked him up from a friend's house, and he looked over at me and said, "Isn't it so great that Joe was such an asshole?"

I look over at him: "What?" He said again, "Isn't it so great that Joe was such an asshole?" Brayden didn't call his dad "Dad" because he wasn't a dad to him. Brayden was only 4½ years old when we left, but he remembers everything. It blows me away how much he remembers from his first years.

This has been a blessing and a curse. A blessing because Brayden understood exactly why we left and had to stay away and stay safe. And a curse because I wish he didn't remember all the pain and suffering that we went through. Brayden had learned over time and saw with his friends and with Pete what a good dad really was and so he called him Joe.

I asked, "What do you mean, specifically?"

"Look at the life we have," he said. "It's amazing. And we wouldn't have it if he wasn't such an asshole."

At that moment, I squealed with joy. For my 17-year-old to see life like that, to appreciate it instead of focusing on growing up without a dad, was a blessing. Every Father's day, no father. Every Christmas, no father. Every game they went to, no father. That was one of the best moments of my life, with Brayden and me counting our blessings that my former husband, his birth father, had been such an asshole.

We have found our happy place. We became free — of the Mission, of being told what to do so excessively, of an abusive husband. I was free to raise my kids the way that I felt was right, without guilt and fear to motivate them.

There are so many gifts. I am fierce. I am strong. I raised two kids, and I did a phenomenal job. I had lots of help, but I did it. So many gifts. My experience with Joe taught me exactly how strong I am. My kids know without a shadow of a doubt that their mama loves them. They know that their mom will do anything for them, period. And that is a gift.

So here's the real test: If I had to do it again, would I? If I had to go through all that trauma and abuse and fear and running, would I do it again? Absolutely. Yes, I would. I would, for my two glorious children alone. The gifts above are extra blessings.

When you cross over from victim to victor, your life changes profoundly. All things open up. You now have the energy to take on things that you never would have taken on. You don't waste time talking about garbage in your life anymore. You live.

I love that I now have the tools not to be a victim. I love that my kids know how not to be a victim. It is a choice, and we don't even have to choose it anymore — we've learned how not to.

Steps and Methods

Here are some suggestions on how you can change perspectives that no longer serve you.

Center yourself and breathe, ask your higher self, the universal intelligence in you, for clarity.

Step 1. Look back on any trauma and ask yourself, "What good has come from this?"

Ask, "Whom do I have relationships with because of this situation?" What major lessons can you take away from this? Who have you helped or who could you help since you have gone through this situation?

See all the good that has come from the situation!

Ask yourself, "Who do you have relationships with because of this situation?"

We've all been through painful, traumatic situations. If I've learned anything over the years, it is that everyone has a story that involves trauma. I encourage you to look at your life and find the hardest thing you've had to deal with. Once you have that in your mind, continue.

Ask, "What major lessons can you take away from this?" Write down anything and everything that you can think of.

Ask, "Who have you helped or who could you help since you have gone through this situation?"

Write down anyone that comes to mind. Keep asking yourself until you have a good list. Write down any little thing that you've been able to do to help other people because you went through your biggest challenge. It is always surprising what comes up. We sometimes forget how our experiences can help others.

Now you should really know and feel the blessings and the people that have come into your life as a result of your life-changing 'negative' experiences.

Step 2. Keep asking the questions until you can answer yes to this question: "If you had to do it over again, would you?"

Ask yourself, "What good has come from this situation?" Write down every little or big thing that has come directly from, or that is indirectly due to, your biggest challenge or pain.

My list includes these blessings:

- My kids know I love them fiercely and that I'll literally do anything for them to protect them.

- I have a beautiful home in Mexico, my happy place, instead of freezing my ass off in Canada. (Sorry, Canadians!)

- I have been able to help so many women find their strength and get them and their kids safe.

- I have a whole new community of friends that I love and adore.

- I now know what it means and feels like to be free!

What good has come from your biggest challenge/pain in your life? Make a good, long, amazing list.

Ask yourself, "If you had to do it over again would you?"

Write down your answer. Seeing it in black and white is quite impactful.

Step 3. No more trauma — what's left is gratitude.

This step helps you feel gratitude when thinking about the trauma, instead of pain.

Celebrate your gratitude!

Celebrate that you are no longer a victim, that you are now a victor! Realize that if you can do that with your biggest challenge, you can do that with anything from your past, as well as anything that may come in your future!

Share this with someone else. It will give them ideas of how to look at things differently.

Understand there is nothing you can't create from a place of pure gratitude. If you can turn your biggest challenge/pain into the biggest gift, there is nothing you can't create that is good.

Now you're learning how to embrace, share the energy of gratitude, and create a new reality.

By performing these steps, you will learn how to see, truly see and understand the phrase, "*Change your perspective, change your life*". You will learn how to look back on any trauma and ask yourself:

- What good has come from this?

- Who do I have relationships with because of this situation?

- What major lessons can I take away from this?

- Who have I helped, or who could I help, since I have gone through the pain?

You will learn how to find gratitude, even for especially hard experiences. This will help you to really know and feel the blessings, and the people, that have come into your life as a result of your trials, and you can get to the point of being willing to do it all again, if necessary. The outcome is to learn how to embrace, share the energy of gratitude, and create a new reality. You will learn just how amazing hard experiences can be, and the massive amounts of gifts that are wrapped up in each one when we train ourselves to look for them.

Go Against the Flow

Sometimes you need to go against the flow, even though it may feel that it could kill you if you do.

Here I will share the story of how I knew I needed to get divorced, even though it went against my culture's rules. When you are facing a challenge like this, it's important to know what the problem is specifically, and to weigh the risks and benefits of making a change that goes against your culture. It's necessary to take action or else go against yourself and feel terrible.

You will also receive steps that can show you what you can do when you have a different perspective and need to go against the flow:

1. Declare the problem.
2. Weigh the risks and benefits.
3. Take action.

When you do these steps, you will get clear on what change needs to happen and the benefits of that change, the pros and cons to making the shift, and how to follow your heart. Being in alignment with yourself is important. Taking risks is the only way out of the bog, but it's worth it!

After leaving my abusive husband, it became evident that there was no way I could or would go back. That meant I had to decide what to do. Stay forever married on paper? Get divorced? What should I do? My culture and my religious beliefs at that time dictated that there was no way I could get divorced. I was 28 years old with two boys, ages 2 and 4, and I believed based on my upbringing, that I didn't have a choice, that I had to be alone forever.

It was difficult to go against everything I had been raised to believe, and to have a few hundred people in my bubble watching me and judging me and making their decisions about me.

But I knew I had to choose differently. And sometimes it's really difficult to do.

The consequence of my getting divorced was that the Mission disowned me. People stopped talking to me, because if they spoke to me they'd be condoning my behavior. This was one of the hardest things that I have ever gone through in my life. The betrayal that I felt from them, the unfair judgment, the incredible aloneness was totally all encompassing for a time. I cried buckets! I went back and forth between whether or not to give my life back to the Mission so that at least I wouldn't be alone.

But the blessing that came from going against the flow is that I have experienced love. Love for myself. I have had partnership and companionship, my boys have had positive male influence in their life. I didn't know what love (in a romantic relationship) was, because I didn't experience love with Joe. Sometimes you need to go against the flow and do what you need to do, what is right for you!

Steps and Methods

Here is how you can learn from my experience.

Center yourself and breathe. Ask your higher self, the universal intelligence in you, for help.

Step 1. Declare the problem. It's important to know what the problem is, specifically.

Ask yourself, "What do I know that I need to do for me and my family, but feel scared or uncertain about it because it goes against the rules of my community, family, or culture?" This can be a tough question to face, so keep breathing through it. Keep asking the question until you have an answer. For me, it was discovering that I needed to get divorced.

Ask yourself, "Why is this important to me?" For me, it was about unconditional love, about freedom, and about living my life according to my own values.

Ask yourself, "If I make a change, what are the benefits?" For me the benefits were hope, companionship, partnership, love, balance, help, happiness, and freedom.

The outcome of this step is to get clear on what change needs to happen and the benefits of that change.

Step 2. Weigh the risks and benefits. It's important to weigh the risks and benefits of making the change that goes against your culture.

Ask yourself, "What are the consequences if I stay true to the rules, or if I don't?"

Write down anything that comes to mind. For me, the consequences weren't small. It may be the same for you.

Ask yourself, "Who else will this choice impact?" Write down any one that comes to mind. My choice impacted my parents the most, as they were leaders in the Mission at the time, and under a tremendous amount of pressure.

Ask yourself, "What decision can I not live with? What can I live with?"

Write down the answers that come to you. At the end of the day, I could not live the rest of my life for a group of other people. I needed to live my life according to *my* values.

The outcome of this step is to get really clear on the pros and cons before making the shift and following your heart.

Step 3. Take action.

It's important to take the necessary action or else go against yourself and feel terrible.

Ask yourself, "What is it that I need or want to do? Be super clear. Fear can creep in, big time. Acknowledge it, and continue with eyes wide open.

Ask yourself, "Who else do I know that has already made the same choice that I could get counsel from, to discover the best possible ways to handle the situation?"

Write down anyone who comes to mind.

Get counsel if possible, and then take action. Schedule time with that person or persons right now to speak with them privately. Make sure you schedule enough time to say all that you need to say and for them to respond. Once you know what to do, go that way.

The outcome of this step is to get some help and take the necessary steps to be in alignment with yourself.

When you follow these steps, you will learn that sometimes you need to go against the flow of your environment. You will learn what your problem is specifically, and to weigh the risks and benefits of making a change that goes against your culture. You will learn that it is necessary to take action, or else you go against yourself and feel terrible. Here are the steps again to recap:

- Declare the problem,
- Weigh the risks and benefits, and then
- Take action.

The hope is that when you do these steps you will get clear on what change needs to happen and the benefits of that change, the pros and cons to making the shift and how to follow your heart. Being in alignment with yourself is important. Taking risks is the only way out of the bog, but it's worth it!

Find a Mentor, Be a Mentor

What if you paid someone to call you out on your shit? To give you a different perspective. That's what I do and have done for years.

Here, I will share the story of finding and hiring Josh, our guru/teacher/coach, and then hiring other coaches for the boys and me. The important thing is to discover what area of your life you need help or support with, and who in your life you could add value to.

It's also important to make sure that you or your kids are learning from the best, a master in the area you need help with. If you are going to teach something, make sure to teach something you are a master at. The importance of this step is to take the leap in hiring a qualified coach so that you can break through where you are stuck and move on to the next level.

I will then share with you the steps on how to do that:

1. Where do you need help? Who could you help?
2. Find a master in that area.
3. Hire them to help you.

Get clear on what areas of your life could use a coach and in what areas of life you can be the coach. You'll learn how to hire and how to call on help to have an impact on your own and others' lives.

I was sick and tired of being sick and tired, of fighting through life alone. Jeremy, my brother, had been suggesting a coach/healer to me. One morning I woke up and I knew that I couldn't go another day without help. Three hours later, I was sitting down with Josh, who has changed the course of the boys' and my life, who has helped me heal. After one hour with Josh, I was bawling my eyes out and I sobbed for an additional four hours. When I left that session, I thought I had lost one whole part of me, I thought and felt that I had been carrying hundreds of pounds, and I didn't even know it until one hundred and ten pounds were released that glorious day.

I saw Josh every week for years, and I had the boys start seeing him, too. Our coaching cost more than my rent, but it was the best thing I could have ever done for my kids. He became a positive role model in their lives.

And God bless Tom Wilhoit, another mentor of mine. He was an older gentleman in Branson, Missouri, and he took me under his wing. Although he was on oxygen, Tom would drive 30 minutes to my house, dragging his oxygen tank with him, and sit at my humble little table. My time in Branson was perhaps the hardest and poorest time in my life, and this man mentored me. He put into my hand CDs of Jim Rohn, *Success* magazine, Wayne Dyer and John Maxwell. Tom Wilhoit warmed me up and got me started on personal development. Then I found Tony Robbins and, wow, did he change my life! I've been to almost every event that he's put out there, and I've taken tons of friends with me, to get mentorship, help, coaching on life, and on how to see life differently.

Get a mentor, be a mentor. This is important. When you're a few chapters ahead of somebody else, you have the right, based on your experience and your knowledge, to help somebody get one step further than they are. Then you get someone who's a few chapters ahead of you, to help you get a few chapters further. Mentorship is one of the most beautiful things I've ever experienced.

I saw that this worked so well that when the boys wanted to learn music, I hired other teenagers to teach them because, again, kids don't want to learn from old fuddy-duddies. They want to learn from kids their age. And so I hired kids who were a few chapters ahead of them on the drums and on the guitar.

So thank you, Giuseppe, a drum prodigy who helped Tate play the drums and took time out of his busy schedule to get Tate started. And Lindan — I thank you for teaching Brayden the guitar, being a friend, and getting him going on what is now my son's career. They are musicians. They are musicians at their core, at their heart. And they got their start from two other teenagers. Amazing.

Then I hired two other guys, a DJ and a busker (someone who plays music in the streets for donations). A Canadian and a Russian, they had moved to Mexico for a few months. I hired them to spend time with the boys and to teach them even more about music and how to present yourself and how to be organized and how to practice and how to rehearse and how to jam. And now my kids can touch almost any instrument and play it.

We hired mentors, we hired teachers, we hired coaches, we hired people who were both masters or a few chapters ahead, and guess what my kids are doing now, at twenty-three and twenty one years old? They are mentoring kids. They are helping others. They are teaching kids music, and about life, and how to get through the divorce of their parents, and how to change perspective, and how to see all the blessings that have come from it. Get a mentor and be a mentor. Trust me, it's worth it.

Steps and Methods

Here is how you can discover what area of your life you need help or support with, and who in your life you could add value to.

Center yourself and breathe. Ask your higher self, the universal intelligence in you and around you, for clarity.

Step 1. Where do you need help? Whom could you help?

To start, ask yourself, "What areas of my life need help?" Write down anything that comes to mind.

Ask yourself, "When I get this help, what would change in my life for the better?" I am putting this together at a writing workshop in Guatemala with a coach named Michael Drew who has helped hundreds of authors get published. He is guiding me on this journey because I have not done this before. It is changing my life for the better because I have help and support, and the book is actually getting done. I have talked about doing this for years, but now it's actually happening. Why? Because I have a professional coach. When you get such mentoring help, what could change in your life for the better?

Ask yourself, "What am I great at, that I could help someone else with?"

Write down anything that comes to mind. I discovered that I am a great teacher, and a great implementer. When I learn something, I implement it right away. I am great with systems and procedures and steps on how to create change.

I love people and I love to inspire. That's why I decided to start coaching officially. I was already coaching in my regular life as people would come up to me and ask me how and what I was doing. But I wanted to do it full-time, because it brings me so much joy.

Ask yourself, "If I coached someone in an area where I'm a master, how could I help impact their lives?" Write down anything that comes to mind.

This step will help you to get clear on what areas of your life could use a coach, and in what areas of life you are capable of being the coach.

Step 2. Find a master in that area.

The importance here is to make sure that you or your kids are learning from the best, a master of that area of which you need help, and to teach that which you're a master of.

Research who you would like to coach you. It's important that you have confidence in them and feel aligned with them. I had read Tony Robbins' book *The Power Within*, and I heard from many different friends how awesome he was. So I felt very excited to go to my first Tony Robbins event.

Get referrals or have enough social proof to feel good about it.

Schedule a first meeting, and see how you feel. Listen to your intuition.

It's wise to schedule a first meeting to see how you feel about your new coach/teacher and make sure it feels good and in alignment with your values.

This step helps you find a coach that is qualified and one you feel comfortable to work with.

Step 3. Hire coaches and mentors to help you.

It's important to take the leap to hiring the coach so that you can break through where you are stuck and move on to the next level.

Figure out your budget. Write down anything that comes to you. I budget for further education because it's that important to me.

Hire the coach. Just do it! A few hours after making my first appointment, I was sitting with my coach, Josh. It might not happen that fast for you, but you get the idea.

Set a time to meet and then re-evaluate. Most relationships need some time to percolate. Give yourself a good shot at transformation and set up coaching for three months to a year. I paid for 20 sessions up front to get started. The more 'skin in the game,' the more you will take it seriously. Trust me. Go all in. You will thank me later.

Do what they ask you to do in the way that they ask you to do it! Listen to your coach. If they ask you to do something, just do it. It's important to expect to be uncomfortable. Here is one of my favorite Tony Robbins sayings: "The more comfortable you can be in the uncomfortable, the better life is!" So get uncomfortable, and get used to it.

When you follow these steps, you will realize how awesome it is to pay someone to call you out on your messes and to learn new things. It's important to discover what area of your life you need help with, and who in your life you could add value to, as well. Following these steps will also help you take the leap to hiring a coach, so you can break through where you are stuck and move on to the next level:

- Where do you need help? Who could you help?
- Find a master in that area,
- Hire them to help you.

You'll get clear on what areas of your life could use a coach, and in what areas of life you are capable of being the coach. You will learn that contributing to a child's/person's life in any way you can is a true blessing and will change and impact your life forever.

In our next chapter, we will look at knowing what you want — so you can plan ways to get it.

 If you'd like further support from me, please use this QR. Looking forward to hearing from you!

Chapter 4

DISCOVERING WHAT YOU REALLY WANT

Wait a second — I actually have a choice? I can actually design my life?

Here, you will learn the importance of knowing what you REALLY want. I will share a story about how a manager of mine shook me up and got me dreaming again. Then I will share with you the steps for achieving your dreams:

1. How to realize you don't have to settle.
2. How to know you have value and are allowed to dream big.
3. How to know what you REALLY want.

Here we will bring out into the open and on paper where in your life you have been settling for less than you want or feel deserving of. You will learn to know your value and what is possible if you want it and to get a very clear idea of what it is that you want to have, be, or experience. Unlike what we have been taught, we actually can choose what we want for our lives!

When I first moved to Mexico, I got a sales position at an amazing new resort. Peter, one of the managers there, was super intense. One day he came up to me and said, "You're so frustrating. You're like this beautiful flower bud that just needs to bloom." I didn't really understand what he was talking about.

"You need to dream," he said. "Do you dream?"
"What do you mean?" I asked.
He asked, "What is your favorite car?"
"I don't know. I've never thought about it.
"OK, that's your homework tonight," he said. "You need to think about what your favorite car is."

Dreaming and Visualizing

I didn't understand about dreaming and about visualizing as a child. I had a really hard time imagining anything that wasn't real and right in front of me. I put all kinds of limitations on what could be. But I asked myself what kind of car I liked. And so the next day I told Peter that I liked Mini Coopers.

He said, "OK, so now you're on the road to getting a Mini Cooper."

I said, "I thought this was just an exercise."

"No," he said, "if you want one, why not have one?"

"Well, they're too expensive," I said. "They're too fancy."

"Amy," he said, "there's nothing wrong with wanting something."

A light went on in my head: It was okay to dream.

I hadn't been taught how to dream. I actually got really excited. "OK, all right, why not? Let's get a Mini Cooper."

The next day, Pete came up to me and said, "I got you a Mini Cooper." He smiled and he handed me a hotwheels car. He had bought me a blue dinky Mini Cooper. I did a little hop of glee.

"Put that on your vision board," he said.

I asked, "What's a vision board?"

"That's a board that you put pictures on, of all the things that you'd like to be and have and places you'd like to go. Then you know what you want, and you move towards it."

This was one of the coolest things I'd ever heard.

Fast forward: I eventually needed to leave Mexico for a while due to the economic crash. I ended up in Missouri. There I bought an old VW bug, a useful, practical car. One day, a friend from work offered to help me get the oil changed. He got into an accident and my car got totaled. I no longer had a car. Later, as I was driving on the highway with a renter that my insurance had given me, I looked up and saw a Mini Cooper dealership. I thought, 'Hmm. Is this possible? Could it be possible? No — they're too expensive. There's no way!'

You have to understand that, in Branson, I had the least money that I've ever had since college. But you never know. So I decided to try. I met with the sales agent, and I used the $5,000 that I got from the insurance for my VW bug crash as a down payment. For $250 a month, I was able to drive out with a Mini Cooper and it was a blue Mini Cooper with British flags on the mirrors.

It was the coolest-looking car I have ever had, ever dreamed of having, or even thought was possible to have. It was such a landmark moment in my life In that moment I started to really dream for the first time. Amazing!

I started believing that things could be different. Not that there was anything wrong with what was going on, but that life could be glorious, that it could be anything that you wanted.

I spent a lot of time on the first vision board that I created, cutting out pictures from magazines and printing photos. Some of the things on it were: go to Africa on a safari, Hawaii, massage chair, take the kids on a Mediterranean cruise. There was a picture from up on the hill in Santorini looking down at a cruise ship. I remember that picture perfectly. It also had something that said, "See a need, fill a need." Which is obvious, but I just wanted to be able to see a need and be able to fill it, to have the money to say, "Oh, you need help, here you go," and not have to say, "Can I afford it?"

I wanted to be able to help in a big way. When I prepared my first vision board, I was living very humbly. And again, there was nothing wrong with that, but I want you to understand that the things that I was putting down were huge stretches for me at the time. I'm proud, humbled, and excited to tell you that everything on that board I have accomplished. I have gone to Africa and done a safari there, and we did that Mediterranean cruise.

I have a similar picture from that same vantage point up on the hill in Santorini, looking down at a cruise ship. It made me so happy to stand there and take that picture. I've been able to help so many people, and I even have a massage chair. Vision boards work! Get specific on what you want, because it's coming. It's coming! Probably in the same shape and color as you put up on your board. When you think about the things that you love, you should get excited about them, and feel the feelings of having that thing or experience as if it has already happened!

Steps and Methods

Here is how you can do it too.

Center yourself and breathe. Ask your higher self, the universal intelligence in you and around "you" for clarity.

1. Realize you don't have to settle.

It's important to accept that you don't need to settle, that you are allowed to dream and dream big!

To start, ask yourself, "Where have I been settling rather than going after my dream?" It's always good to take inventory and see where you are settling.

Ask yourself, "What do I have to believe in order to allow myself to settle in this way?" Write down anything that comes to mind, without judgment.

Ask yourself, "What are the consequences of these beliefs?" In my case the consequence of thinking that dreaming was materialistic is why I didn't dream and instead settled.

Bring out into the open and on paper where in your life you have been settling for less than you want or feel deserving of.

Step 2. Know you have value and are allowed to dream big.

It's important to change your psychology so that you can feel worthy to dream.

Realize you have work to do in this area of worth. Say to yourself, "I have some work to do in this area of worth, and of feeling deserving!" Awareness is the first step! We have to actually wake up to be able to make the change.

Surround yourself with people who build you up and think big. If you don't have people in your life who are building you up and encouraging you to have big dreams, then find some.

Read books and listen to podcasts from those who have accomplished what they set out to accomplish. This will build your belief up. You need to build the belief that you are worthy, that it's okay to dream, and that you can dream big!

This step can help you know your value and what is possible, if you want it enough.

Step 3. Know what you REALLY Want.

Get into a situation where you can achieve your goals/dreams. Get into a great state of mind by playing some inspiring music. Find a quiet place to sit where there are no distractions. Move your body while listening to the music and think of at least three things you are thankful for.

Then ask yourself what you want. Write down anything that comes to mind and keep repeating the question until you have at least 10 things on your list. It's important that you don't filter your answers.

Ask yourself, "What do I really want? Who do I really want to be? How do I want to feel?"

Write down anything that comes to mind and keep repeating the questions until you have answers for all three of them.

Ask yourself, "Why do I want it?"

Write down a long list! I usually give a page in my notebook for each item that I desire and then under that I write all the whys. The longer the list, the more important it is to you.

The outcome of this step is to get a very clear idea of what it is that you want to have, be, or experience.

When you follow these steps, you will learn that you actually have a choice, that you can actually design your own life. You don't have to settle for less than what you really want. You can dream big. By changing your psychology, you can feel worthy to dream.

To recap, you have these steps to move yourself forward:

- Realize you don't have to settle for less.
- Know that you have value and are allowed to dream big.
- Know what you *REALLY* want.

The outcome is to bring out into the open and on paper where in your life you have been settling for less than you want or feel deserving of. Unlike what we have been taught, we actually can choose what we want for our lives! It's time to design *YOUR* life!

We Do More to Avoid Pain than Move Toward Pleasure

What are the consequences if you don't make the change? Sigmund Freud says we will do more to avoid pain than to move toward pleasure. So what if you understand the consequences of not being true to yourself? What if you could decide and choose, consciously, what it is that you want to believe? The important thing is to give yourself permission to live your life!

I explore this here by sharing my story of how I gave myself permission to get divorced, to date again and have pre-marital sex, and to develop my own belief system instead of the biblical upbringing I was brought up on. I will then share with you the steps on how to have a grasp of the cost and pain if you don't go after what you want with these steps:

1. What will happen if I don't make the change?
2. Decide if you are willing to live with these questions.
3. Do whatever you have to do for you — It's *your* life.

Doing all this helps you to make an informed decision and give yourself full permission to live and enjoy your life, no matter what anyone else thinks. By seeing and feeling the pain of the consequences of not living your life, it will help motivate you to live the life that you want.

When you start asking yourself what you want, you see things you haven't before. You may see you haven't been living your truth. We do more to avoid pain than to even move toward pleasure.

I have found this to be true, as I mentioned before, especially in thinking about getting a divorce and leaving my career as a missionary, because for me that was the same thing. By getting a divorce, I would HAVE to leave the Mission. This was terribly painful and difficult as most of my community disowned me, and yet it ultimately freed me when I decided not to go back to Joe and to leave the Mission.

There are some consequences to doing things differently, and I found out the second I started dating again. And wow! The backlash! I even had people from the Mission reporting to my father, questioning which change room I was changing in, in the hockey arena, accusing me of changing my clothes in a room with another man, which didn't happen. So I made my own choice. I have my own relationship with God directly; I don't need men to tell me what God is telling me.

One of the biggest shifts I've made is that I no longer live my life entirely or literally based on what the Bible says. Here is my issue with the Bible: It was written by men inspired by God. Men (all humans) are notoriously full of imperfection and the ungodly need for control and power over others. Therefore there could be some things in the Bible not of God. I also believe the Universe's/God's love is unconditional—completely unconditional—in that there is nothing that I need to do or believe in order to be more His kid. I am a child of the Universe/God and I am loved unconditionally, period. In addition, we all have God in us, and I feel as well that I have been led by Source/God to do this book. I continuously ask what I should share and what I should not. We can be led by God in us, by the Holy Spirit, by Source, by Intuition or whatever you want to call it — we can be led by that. And so I made a decision to live my own life, led by Source/God in me.

Steps and Methods

Here's how you can learn how to get to the point of living YOUR life too.

Center yourself and breathe. Seek counsel from your higher self, the universal intelligence in you.

Step 1. What will happen if I don't make the change? What are the consequences?

Ask yourself, "What are the consequences if I'm not true to myself?"

Write down anything that comes to mind, without judgment. (If I hadn't gotten divorced or changed my beliefs about premarital sex, I would still feel guilty and ashamed.)

Ask yourself, "Who else will be affected if I don't follow my truth?"

Write down anyone that comes to your mind. (For me, it was my kids.)

Visualize yourself at the end of your life and look back on how it might look if you are not true to yourself. How would it be for you if you don't live your truth?

The outcome of this step is to have a grasp of the cost and pain if you don't go after what you want.

Step 2. Decide: are you willing to live with these consequences?

Weigh out the pros and cons of your choice. Write down whatever comes to mind, without judgment. For me, the pros to living my truth is that I'm actually living MY truth. It creates freedom and immense joy and beautiful experiences. The cons: I lost almost my whole community of friends. What are the pros and cons to living your truth or doing what is expected of you?

Get outside feedback from a coach or mentor or someone you trust. This is another perspective, so you can see things from a different vantage point.

Make your choice. If everything in your body is rejecting the answer, then you need to ask again until you find the answer you can live with, and it feels good in your body and mind.

This step helps you get to a position of being able to make an informed decision.

Step 3. Do whatever you have to do for you. It's your life.

The importance of this step is to give yourself permission to live your life!

Give yourself permission to live your life. You are allowed. It's yours. I'm so glad that I did! My kids thank me often for raising them in the way that I did. Give yourself permission to live your life. Say it out loud.

Get excited to live your life. No guilt. The next step is easy — celebrate! Celebrate your sovereignty! This party can take as long as you want!

Start living it! It's important to let the people who are affected by your choice know how you feel and why. Give them time to adjust. Try not to let their reaction affect you. They may not ever understand, either. That's okay — they don't have to. They get to live their life, now it's your turn to live yours. Start living it! Enjoy!

This step helps you give yourself full permission to live and enjoy your life, no matter what anyone else thinks. It will naturally allow you to let others live their lives as well.

If you follow these steps, you will understand the consequences of not being true to yourself. You will know how to decide and choose, consciously, what it is that you want to believe—and give yourself permission to live your life! You learned the steps on how to grasp the cost and pain if you don't go after what you want:

- What will happen if I don't make the change?
- Decide — are you willing to live with these consequences?
- Do whatever you have to do for you. It's your life.

Doing these things will help you make an informed decision and give yourself full permission to live and enjoy your life, no matter what anyone else thinks. By seeing and feeling the pain of the consequences of not living your life, it will help motivate you to live the life that you want. It has been the most glorious thing, finding that ability to be free. Freedom is glorious!

Make the Main Thing the Main Thing

What makes you smile the biggest? What if you reviewed your list of dreams and made sure they were really your dreams and not someone else's for you? What if you had an idea of when you would like these dreams to come to be? What if you knew why your most important dreams were so important to you, so you could focus on them first?

Here I will share with you how I created my dream list. I will share how I figured out what I wanted, why I wanted it, and how I mapped it all out!

You will also learn steps on how to do this yourself:

1. Make a list of dreams and make sure that what's on the list is YOUR list and no one else's.

2. Write down how long it will take to realize each dream.

3. Pick your top three in year one, and write down "why" you want to have or accomplish that.

These steps will help you to be super sure about your dreams and that you are living yours — and yours alone! If you are in a committed relationship go through this process individually, then come together and figure out how you can honor both of your dreams. You will also be clear and know the time frame of each dream and therefore the order in which they will happen and which ones to focus on first. You will be so clear on what lights you up and what makes you jump out of bed in the morning.

One day I went to the beach in Mexico, sat down, listened to inspiring music, and began to write. I started writing down whatever it is that made me smile and lit me up — ways that I wanted to be, things that I wanted to have, places I wanted to go, things I wanted to learn — anything and everything that I could think of for the near future and far future, that made me smile with my soul!

I didn't filter. I looked at the list and I wondered how many of these dreams were actually mine or whether they were simply things that people told me I should do. The point is to make sure that you're stoked about whatever's on your list. I was excited with my list by the time I was done on that beach that day.

On that list was having my own house, and I thought that this dream would be a long-term dream, I did not think it was going to happen any time soon. But I wrote down that I wanted a house. And I wrote down where I wanted it and that I wanted it to have a view of the ocean. I got specific on how I wanted it.

When you start writing things down and you get clear on what you want, magic starts happening. I'm not kidding you.

Only God and I knew what was on my list. Two weeks later, my friend Bobby said to me, "I have land and I want to sell you half." I realized this was God delivering exactly what I wanted. And the land was in the exact place I wanted! I asked, "Can you see the ocean?" He put a picture in front of me that showed the view.

I told him I didn't have money. But he said I could buy it in installments. This is rare, because in Mexico you pay cash for houses, because interest rates are astronomical. We figured out what worked best for us. Two weeks earlier, I had written, "I want to have my own house," and four weeks later I had my own lot! We drew up the papers within a week or two and I had the land. I had the land, and it was mine.

The next step was to build. I thought I'd have the land and eventually build on it. I'd written my dream list in January. In May, a good friend of mine came to me and said, "I'm ready."

"Ready for what?"

"To start building your house. I have a contractor."

I told him that I didn't have enough money for that. He asked, "Do you have some money?" I told him yes, and he said, "Okay, we'll just start with what you have and when it runs out, we'll stop." 'Viva Mexico!' I thought. We started building.

Brick by brick, I was able to keep going week by week, paycheck to paycheck. Somehow we were always able to keep going. The boys and I moved into our house before Christmas. Only eleven-and-a-half months earlier, I had decided I wanted it, and now I had it. So it works to know clearly what you want — and then watch the magic!

Steps and Methods

Here is how you can learn how to dream big too.

Center yourself, breathe, and seek clarity from your higher self.

Step 1. Make a list of dreams and make sure that what's on the list is YOUR list and no one else's dreams. Write down anything that comes to mind. I wanted to build my own house. What do you really want? Who do you really want to be? How do you want to feel? Go over your list from earlier and add anything else that comes to mind.

Scratch off any "dream list" items that don't light you up and make you physically smile when you think about them.

Ask yourself, "What do I really want to have, feel, be, experience, do, and accomplish in my life?" It's important to ask multiple times to get through the layers of your mind and heart to find the truth.

This step helps you to be super sure about your dreams and that you are living yours and yours alone! When I left the beach that day with my fresh list of dreams, I was buzzing with anticipation and expectation. Make sure you are excited about your list of dreams and goals.

Step 2. Write down how long each one will take to come into being. Review your list again.

Without being overly analytical and thinking about how, write a number next to each dream representing the time for it to come to pass. So if you want to see it come to fruition this year, put a 1 in front of it. If you think it will take two years, write down the number two, etc. Many things on your list are likely to happen sooner than you think. That has often been my experience, as with the land I bought.

The outcome is to know the time frame of each dream and therefore the order in which they will happen and which ones to focus on first.

Step 3. Pick your top three in year one, and write down why you want to have or accomplish that. Look at your list of dreams for the first year. Take your list and separate the dreams and goals that you want to accomplish this year and put them into a separate list. You want to get clear on what you are aiming for during the next 12 months.

Highlight the top three that you are the most excited about. Put a star next to the top three things on that list.

Add "why" under each one til you have a long list of whys. There should be a LONG list under each item. "The bigger the why, the easier the how," said entrepreneur Jim Rohn. So make a long list.

The outcome of this step is to have your top three dreams and their whys clear as a bell so there is nothing that can take you off course from making it happen.

When you follow these steps, you will have your list of dreams and they will be really your dreams and not someone else's dream for you. You will know when you would like these dreams to come true, the most important dreams, and why they are so important to you, just like I created my dream list!

You also have the steps on how to do this yourself:

- Make a list of dreams and make sure that what's on the list is YOUR list, and no one else's.
- Write down how long for each one to come to fruition.
- Pick your top three in year one, and write down why you want to have or accomplish that.

These steps will help you to be sure about knowing and living your dreams.

You will also be clear and know the time frame of each dream, and therefore the order in which they will happen and which ones to focus on first. You will be so clear on what lights you up, what makes you jump out of bed in the morning, that nothing will stop you from going out and making it happen.

Next we will look at planning your life.

 If you'd like further support from me, please use this QR. Looking forward to hearing from you!

Chapter 5

PLANNING WITHOUT ACTION IS FUTILE

Move your ass, NOW! Planning without action is futile. It's important to know what you want and then to break it down to figure out how to get there.

Here I'm exploring taking things one step at a time. Action is key — or your dream is nothing but a thought. To illustrate this, I will share with you a story about how I had a dream to build my parents a home and how I was able to make that happen.

You will also learn the steps that I took, so you can do it as well:

1. Know what you want.
2. Achieve one chunk at a time.
3. Do it!

These steps will help you remember to review your dream before taking massive action and get clear on all the benefits, so that you stay on course. You will also discover that when you take things one step at a time, you actually see it come to fruition while enjoying the journey!

One of the dreams on my list was to build a home for my mom and dad. They are two of the best people that exist on this planet, and they have given their hearts and their souls to the people that they have served for years in the Mission that I grew up in.

They are so friendly and filled with heart that we were always the last people out of the church. They were flown all over the planet to speak, and people would fight to be in their presence. They are beautiful. Because they were missionaries, money was tight. With our Mission, churches and friends support the missionaries by sending them money every month. During my missionary years, I wrote an average of 20 thank-you notes a month for the support given us. But sometimes money is tight, and it's a little hard to save and prepare for the future. So my dream was to build them a house.

I got a contractor and we started building. When you place things on your dream list, things happen because you know why you want them. I wanted my parents to have a happy retirement. I wanted them not to worry ever again about how they were going to put food on the table. I wanted them to be able to go out to eat if they wanted, to not have to order off the dollar menu, to go to nice restaurants. I wanted them to be 'footloose and fancy free'!

For years we lived in housing that was provided by the Mission so I wanted them to be able to decorate and pick out everything about the house. My parents are gifted at interior design and can turn a cheap shack into a castle. So I wanted them to have their own mansion, their own estate, their own little kingdom.

I hired the contractor and week by week, we looked at what would come next — how much we'd need for each step. This meant I'd have to close more sales or do more volume or work late — whatever was needed. I did it to have the money for this dream.

Week by week, brick by brick, I built this beautiful home for my parents. The day that they drove in and saw their home was one of the happiest days of my life. It's a full two-bedroom house with a huge terrace, from which they can see the ocean and the whales breach. What a joy to be able to provide that for them and to experience and receive the gratitude that comes with it.

It's such a cool thing to know what you want and why you want it, and then to go after it — and then to finally enjoy it!

Steps and Methods

Here is how you can plan your action steps like I did.

Center yourself and breathe. Ask your higher self, the universal intelligence available to you, for clarity.

Step 1. Know what you want.

Go through your list of wants again, and ask yourself, "What do I want?" Write down anything else that comes to mind and keep repeating the question until you have at least 10 things on your list. It's important that you don't filter your answers, don't judge them — just answer whatever lights you up.

Ask yourself, "Why do I want it?"

Continue to write a list of whys under each "want." The longer the list, the more important it is to you. It's important to go over your list at least a couple times to get very clear on your dreams.

Ask yourself, "How will I feel when I get it?" Write down anything that comes to mind.

The outcome of this step is that before taking massive action, you review your dream and get totally clear on all the benefits and whys so that you stay on course.

Then it's important to visualize your completed dream, and feel the emotion of that day!

Step 2. Achieve one chunk at a time.

Ask yourself, "What do I need to do first to get this done?"

Write down anything that comes to mind. For me, it was to find a contractor. I had already made plans for the whole property for my parents when I had purchased it years earlier. What is your first step to getting what you want accomplished?

Ask yourself, "What else can I do now"?

This seems obvious, but a lot of times the obvious isn't that obvious to us. We tend to make things harder than they actually are.

Know that when you take things one step at a time, you will actually see it come to fruition bit by bit and you will enjoy the journey.

Step 3. Do it!

Take action, or the dream stays only a thought.

Put one foot in front of the other. Once you know what needs to be done next, then do it.

If you can't do it now then schedule it right now for a time that you can do it. When you schedule it, then it's as good as done. The key is to keep putting one foot in front of the other. Without action, your dream remains merely an idea. So achieve whatever step you can do right now.

Commit to following through and finishing. Make a conscious choice to follow through on whatever it is that you want to see come to fruition. Many times people quit after a few roadblocks. Be different. Stick to the plan.

Play full-out. No half-assed efforts.

You don't want to just squeak over the finish line — you want to finish well. So play full-out. Play this game with all your heart! This is your life. If you won't play it with all of your heart, who will?

Review your whys often!

Review your list to make sure what you're working on comes to fruition. The more you remember why, the less likely you will be tempted to quit or get discouraged.

Remember: The bigger the why, the easier the how!

This step helps you see your dreams through to completion!!!

By following these steps, you will learn that planning without action is futile. It's first important to know what you want and then take things one step at a time. Action is key, or else your dream will stay nothing but a thought. Remember the story of how I had a dream to build my parents a home and how I made that happen, step by step, week by week.

To recap:

1. Know what you want.
2. Achieve one chunk at a time.
3. Do it!

This will help you know that before taking massive action, you need to review your dream and get clear on all the benefits and whys so you stay on course. You will also discover that when you take things one step at a time, you actually see it come to fruition, while enjoying the journey! So move your ass — *now!*

You can read in my blogs about how I pushed through my fears and limiting beliefs and took my kids on an around the world tour. We experienced 13 countries in 64 days!

Shoulder-to-shoulder in planes, trains, boats, rickshaws, tuk tuks, motorcycles, four wheelers and automobiles: the four of us got to have the trip of a lifetime! (Zander was the fourth person, my third son, whom I unofficially adopted when he was 16 and raised til 19—you can read more about him and how he came to join our family on my website under Blogs titled - "It Takes A Village.")

Our trip around the world is also too expansive to write here but you can find it on my website under Blogs, titled, "13 Countries 64 Days"! You'll discover what it took for us to pull off this trip of a lifetime, and what we got to experience and enjoy.

Ride the Carousel of Life

When your life is out of balance, it's like trying to drive a car with only three tires. Balance is a wonderful thing, so let's do what we can to stay balanced.

Here I'm going to share the nine areas you should focus on in life. Yes, nine things. You'll see that by spending your time and energy on them you'll create an outstanding life. I'll also show you how to get specific on where to implement change.

To illustrate this, let me share a story with you about how I have consciously worked on these nine areas, highlighting the balancing of my male and female energies.

I'll also give you these steps to find balance and happiness:

1. Learn the nine areas in life to focus on and where you are in each category.
2. Ask what you need to do to get from where you are now to where you want to be — and why.
3. Get specific as to how, what, where, when, and why you'll make changes.

Doing these steps will allow you to know exactly where you are on the map of your life in regards to these nine areas. You will learn how to create a list of things to do or be to enhance and fill out your Wheel, and therefore your life.

As a result, you will train your mind to get specific on the changes you want to see so that your mind knows exactly what it wants. When you focus on these nine things in life, your path will be smoother. You will be able to make the necessary adjustments to create the balance in your life that you've always wanted!

The Wheel of Life

I will never forget the day I was introduced to the concept of the Wheel of Life assessment tool. The Wheel of Life is based on the notion that specific categories or areas of focus form the cornerstone of your overall life experience, which works with basic human needs.

I have since created my own Wheel of Life. It's made up of the nine things that I feel are important for me to pay attention to in my life. When I filled out that pie chart and realized that I was running on bumpy tires, completely out of balance, I knew it was time to get my shit together.

Pay attention to these nine things — and thankfully there are only nine, not thirty. The one piece of the pie chart that really blew me away was the importance of balancing male and female energy. It doesn't matter what your sexual orientation is, there's a male energy and a female energy in each individual and in each relationship.

This is *not* something I was taught. I've discovered that most people haven't been taught this, either. I've noticed that the current program in society and on this planet is the overmasculation of the females and the emasculation of the males.

We are seeing more and more men who are more feminine than their natural core would be, and women more masculine than their natural core would be, and it's messing things up. Without things in balance, there are consequences, there are backlashes. And this really became known to me when I was at Date With Destiny, an amazing course with Tony Robbins. At one point, he said, "I'm going to yell a word, and I want you to do whatever you feel led to do when you hear me say this word."

There were 5,000 people in the room. Tony shouted, "Freedom!" And around 2,500 men, and me, stood up to yell, "Ahhhh!" Like something out of Braveheart. I looked around and saw that I was the only female doing this. It made total sense to me. I sat down and thought, 'Holy shit! This is why I haven't had the relationship that I want. I'm always the man in the relationship!" Remember, I had been a tomboy, and proud of it, and I was proud not to need a man.

I can now see that I created this "I don't need a man" thing, all while actually wanting a man. I realized that this was something I had to really work on, even though everything in me resisted this. I needed and wanted to honor the feminine in me.

I've since learned that it's totally possible to be a badass and still be in your feminine. It's back and forth. We have both energies in us. It's really a matter of just calling on the energy that we need at the right time.

I'm still learning so much about it. In that moment of standing up and roaring with the men, I knew I had to do something, and I knew I couldn't do it on my own.

Among my acquaintances was a beautiful badass, super feminine woman. We barely knew each other, but I decided to approach her. I said, "I see you as a badass, feminine goddess. Would you be willing to mentor me?" She looked at me sideways, and then said, "Yeah!"

I didn't know how this was going to work because she lived in Texas. But my intuition said she was the one. "Ask her, do it now, don't delay!" I told myself. And so I did. The most beautiful, magical thing happened. She called me up about a month later and said, "I want to introduce you to a women's group." And I thought, "Hell no!"

I had a strict rule: No more than one or two women at a time. No baby showers, no bridal showers. Too many women in one place, and I just couldn't handle it. "Trust me," she said. I agreed because I knew I needed help. And it has been a transformational experience.

I am now surrounded by the most amazing badass feminine goddesses that I could ever imagine. They are helping me see that in myself as well. So I am so thankful for this understanding of paying attention to the female and male energies.

Steps and Methods

Here is how you do it:

Step 1. Record nine areas in life to focus on and where you are in each.

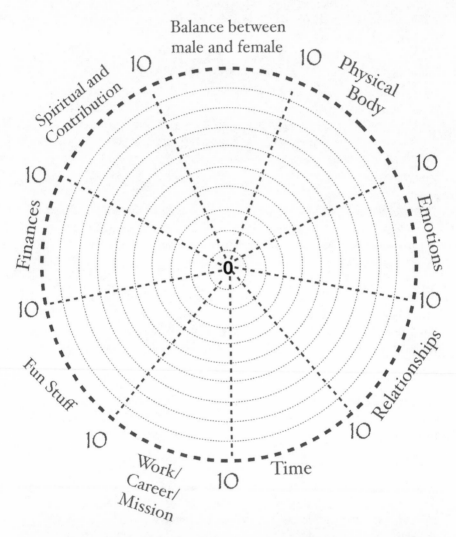

Lay out your nine subjects. There are specific subjects to focus on that make up the Wheel of Life. There are many sets of subjects out there that you can find. The subjects I use here are the ones I've created for myself.

In my experience, these are the nine things you have to focus on to have an exceptional, extraordinary, amazing life:

- Physical Body/Health
- Emotions/Meaning
- Relationships
- Career/Mission
- Time
- Fun Stuff
- Finances
- Spiritual/Contribution
- Balance of Male and Female Energy

Center yourself, breathe, and ask your higher self, the universal intelligence in you and around you, for the truth.

Make a copy or draw the Wheel of Life onto a piece of paper and fill in the categories just like the graphic shown above. On lined paper, write out a discussion of your strengths and weaknesses for each of the nine subjects. (Writing out your thoughts on paper is a proven technique that helps you grasp your own ideas more clearly and evaluate them more accurately.)

First discuss your health and how you feel in your body and about your body. How do you feel you are doing physically?

Next, discuss your emotions: how do you feel about your day? Your life? Your emotions? Are you in control of them or not? Or do they control you?

Next up is relationships: Do you have great relationships? Do you have constant trouble with relationships? What does that look like?

Next is time: How do you manage your time? Do you feel that you have no time or do you know that you are managing it well with schedules?

Work/Career/Mission make up your next piece of the pie: Are you doing what you love? Do you feel fulfilled? Are you doing well in your work

Then comes Fun Stuff: Are you doing anything for fun, or are you doing too much for fun and other things aren't being taken care of?

Then there are your finances: How are you doing financially, in comparing where you are and where you want to be?

Spiritual/Contribution: This doesn't necessarily mean going to church; this means your connection to Source, to the universe, to God. How are you doing? Are you taking any action? Are you doing anything to enhance that relationship? Are you contributing to the planet? Are you helping out?

Last, but not least, is balancing male and female energies.

Everyone has male energy and female energy. I was more in my masculine. I had the masculine energy tapped in because of my upbringing and my story of trying to feel valued. I felt that women weren't valued, and I definitely felt that I wasn't valued. So I set out to prove that I could do whatever a guy could do, and I could do it better. That energy is masculine. Whether you're a man or a female, that's a masculine energy.

The female energy is more in the flow of things. The male energy is solid and secure, like redwood trees, and the female energy, like bamboo, moves and flows and changes. It doesn't matter if it's two men or two woman or not. If it's not polarized, you have a problem. Sometimes a person is more masculine, one's more feminine. And that's how you keep the attraction.

Same with men and women in relationships. Even in yourself, the male-female energy is there. You need both. There is a time to flow. There is a time to follow. And then there is a time to be a warrior. So it is learning the art of going back and forth into those energies and calling on that energy when you need it.

For example, "I need my warrior energy right now" or "no, now is not the time, I need to be in my flow." That's what I mean by the male-female energy for that piece of the pie.

Measure where you are in each category. Be kind, but also honest with yourself.

Ask yourself, "Where am I on a scale of one to ten in my physical body?" This means health.

As shown in the Wheel of Life graphic on page 74, draw a line from the 0 in the center out to each of the nine subject names, and put a "10" on the end of each line; draw 10 equally spaced concentric circles overlaying each slice of the pie. Now, if you think you're probably a seven in Physical Body/Health, fill in (darken) the 7 sections in that section of the pie all the way from the "0" center out through the 7th segment (see example on page 78); do the same with the other slices of your Wheel of Life — and be honest, yet kind, as you fill in for each slice from the center out for the right number of segments.

This is just figuring out where we are on a map. When we know where we are, we can know where we're going. This is the beauty of the Wheel of Life.

For Emotions, ask yourself, "Am I in control of my emotions or do they control me?"

How are you doing with your emotions and how do you feel about your life in general? Are you happy? Are you sad? When you know the number, draw a line under the number and fill in back to the center, and be kind and honest with yourself.

For each wedge or slice of the Wheel of Life pie, decide on a number and then shade and fill in from that line back to zero, to the center of the Wheel.

Ask yourself, "How am I doing in my relationships?" Be kind and honest with yourself.

Time. Ask yourself, "Where do I run out of time? What is my time like?"

Work. Ask yourself, "How do I feel about work, career, or my life's mission?" Do you like what you do? Do you feel fulfilled? Are you doing well? If you take all those things into consideration, where do you stand? Ask the question, decide on a number, and fill in/shade in back to the center of the Wheel.

Finances. How are you doing financially in comparison to where you've been and where you'd like to be? Can you take care of your needs? Is it a struggle?

Where are you when it comes to fun stuff? Are you making intentions to have fun and to do things?

Spirituality and contribution. What are you doing to feed the spiritual side of yourself? Are you honoring that at all? Are you contributing to the planet? Are you contributing to another human being? How? Sometimes people don't know that this is something they should focus on.

How are you balancing your male and female sides? Are you aware of them? Are you calling the male energy when you need it? Are you calling the female energy when you need it? Is this something you need to work on?

How does your Wheel look? Is it big, full and round, or is it jagged and uneven? I don't know anyone who's done this the first time and come up with a balanced Wheel. You can't measure what you don't manage. That's why this tool is amazing. It helps you see exactly where you are.

You can manage what you measure. Now you know that there are nine things to manage, and we just measured them, so in three months or so from now, go back to this and ask these same questions on a new pie chart for your Wheel of Life. Once the new one is completed, compare them and you will see progress, and progress equals happiness.

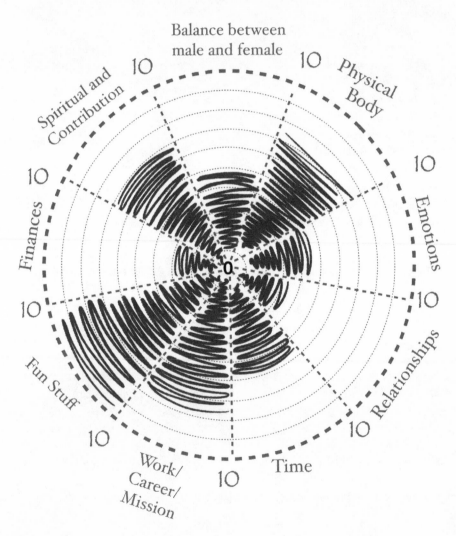

Step 2. Ask, "What do I need to do to get from where I am to where I want to be, and why? What steps do I need to take?"

Ask yourself, "What do I need to get from where I am, to where I want to be?"

Create habits and systems that keep you on track.

Here's how I start my day: I drink a glass of water and do a yoga routine. I take a walk and I listen to my affirmations about how amazing, kind and loving I am.

Ask yourself several questions to gain focus as you go around the Wheel again:

- What do I have to research?
- What do I have to do?
- Who do I need to be?
- How do I want to feel?
- How often, with whom?
- Where do I want my finances to be?
- How do I want to feel at work?
- What kind of work environment do I want?

It starts with you. We are all responsible for our own lives.

Ask these questions regarding your male and female sides:

- What do I need to do to boost my male energy?
- What do I need to do to boost my female energy?
- What course should I take?
- What sport should I do in order to develop even more the male or female energy?

Both sides are needed, both are necessary. Both are magic. Flowing is magic, being firm and certain and strong is magic. They are both needed.

Keep going around the wheel. If you get stuck, move on and come back to it later. Remember that you have a page for each slice of the pie. You can build on it and get clear on it.

When you ask a good question, you get a good answer. When you ask an outstanding question, you get an outstanding answer. And these are amazing questions.

- What steps do I need to take?

Put your Wheel in a place where you can see it every day.

As you go about your day, ask yourself,

- What can I do today towards this?
- What can I do today towards that?
- What could I do at the same time?

Just keep asking yourself, "What steps do I take next, towards living a balanced life?"

Create a list of things to do or be to enhance and fill out your personal Wheel of Life — and therefore your life.

Step 3. Get Specific.

Ask yourself, "What do I need to do?"

Go through your Wheel a third time and get even more specific by asking this question for each slice of the pie:

Ask yourself, "Where do I need to go to complete X?"

Go through the Wheel again and make sure you have asked and answered the question, if appropriate. This process is to make sure you have the details.

Go through the Wheel again and make sure you have asked and answered the question for each slice of the pie. For example, "How long will I exercise everyday?" This process is to make sure you have the details in there.

Ask yourself, "With whom will I be doing X?"

Make sure you have asked and answered this question for each slice of the pie, if appropriate.

- How much will it cost?

By following these steps, you will train your mind to get specific on the change you want to see so that your mind knows exactly what it wants.

When you follow these steps, you will discover that balance is a wonderful thing! That there are only nine things to focus on in life and that by putting time and energy toward them creates an outstanding life.

You will also learn how to get very specific as to how, what, where, and when you will make these changes, as I did in balancing my male and female energies. You learned the steps to take and questions to ask yourself so that you can find balance, and happiness, too:

- Make a Wheel of Life to record the nine areas in life you want to focus on, and record where you are in each category,
- Ask, "What do I need to do to get from where I am to where I want to be and why? What steps do I need to take?"
- Get specific as to how, what, where, when, and why you will do these changes.

How do you find balance and freedom with your finances?

Your life cannot be in balance if you don't have your finances in balance. I have a system that works — and that enabled me to realize my dream list. This system saved my life. I don't know how I would have been able to raise two kids alone, given some of the circumstances we found ourselves in. But this system works. You can read all about it on my website, under blogs titled "Financial Freedom."

How do you find balance and freedom with your health? If you don't have your health, you don't have much. Focus on these four categories for your health:

- Your mind
- Water
- Food
- Exercise

I have a lot of information on what I've done, filled with recommendations, that you can find on my website. You'll see them under blogs titled "Health and Happiness."

So, when you work with your Wheel of Life, you will discover how to create a list of things to do or be, which will enhance your life.

Next we will look at dealing with fear.

 If you'd like further support from me, please use this QR. Looking forward to hearing from you!

Chapter 6

FEAR IS A BITCH UNTIL YOU LEARN TO TAKE IT WITH YOU

What if you learned to dance with fear?

In this section, I explore how you should focus on what you desire, not what you fear. Fear is a normal human condition. It's never going to go completely away. That's why you need to learn how to dance with it, to take it with you, and to visualize what you want as if it is already complete.

To illustrate this, I will share the story of the fear of being almost in a helicopter crash and how I had to take care of a tribal man's finger after I watched him cut it off in front of me. Then you will learn what I did so that you, too, can make the best of *everything* and visualize the outcome that you want:

1. Keep your eye on the prize
2. Take fear with you.
3. Create your own mental movie.

You will learn to not let fear win. The mind is powerful. You will learn the amazing skill of learning how to use fear as fuel, to use it to help you get to wherever you are going!

Has fear ever stopped you from doing what you want to do? It sure has done so to me! Fear can be a real bitch sometimes. But we have to learn how to work with it. Fear is human, but it doesn't have to rule us.

Once, I had to deal with fear when we were flying into the tribe. It was my son Brayden's first time going in with us. He was one year old. We had our little jungle camp set up. Now, it was time to bring in Brayden. We were in a helicopter, because that was the only way to get into the tribe. That tribal village was one of the most primitive, most remote villages on the planet. It took a small Cessna 206 airplane an hour over the mountains to meet up with a helicopter and then we took that the rest of the way into the tribe.

It was another 20-minute ride over the jungle that looked like heads of broccoli for miles and miles. I was in the back of the helicopter with Brayden on my lap, my husband, Joe, was up in the front with the pilot, and beside me were all of our supplies: chainsaws, gasoline, shovels, axes, food, diapers, and all the things we needed to start a life there in the tribe. Things were going along fine when all of a sudden, whoo, whoo, whoo... all these sirens started going off. So many different bells and whistles! It was very clear very quickly that we were in trouble.

The pilot had lots of hours under his belt, and he instinctively knew somehow not to put it into auto rotate, which is what they normally do in a situation like that. The pilot was dealing with the helicopter, and I was trying to deal with my fear. I had Brayden on my lap, and my brain was telling me to freak out. I countered this by asking myself how I could act to make sure we would survive — brace for impact, use supplies, etc.

We landed that helicopter on a piece of sandbar in the middle of a river that was probably three feet by six feet long, placing the rails of the helicopter sideways across the little peninsula. The rails were hanging over the edge on either side. We got out of the helicopter, so thankful to be alive!

But we were in the middle of the jungle, and were not done surviving, yet. And sure enough, there's a tent pitched nearby. Two guys get out. One was burnt from head to toe, because he had been blown up in an IRA bomb in Ireland. He was there as the bodyguard for the other gentleman, who was panning for gold. And so Dave, our helicopter pilot, told us he'd take the helicopter back to be repaired.

We sat and had tea with these two Irish dudes in the middle of the jungle, and I even got to hold gold nuggets in my hand from gold that they found in the streams. We didn't know when he was coming back, or if he was coming back, actually. But sure enough, we finally heard the helicopter coming, and he landed back down on that tiny little sandbar! We loaded back up and headed the rest of the way into the jungle.

It was something else. My heart was in my throat. I can hardly believe that we had just gone through that.

Another example of having to face and take fear with me was when a woman in the village passed away after a tree fell on her, crushing her skull. She was the mother of Roni, one of the main guys in our tribe who was working with us to help us learn the language. This woman had lived in another village a day's hike away. This was the first death in the village for us. It was important for us to know and understand how the people in this tribe mourned their dead. We wanted to respect their customs and support them. Joe and I, with a member of the tribe carrying Brayden in a pack on his back, started out to the village. We had what we needed to spend the night. We had to cross big logs across rivers and traverse mountain terrain. Not even twenty minutes into the hike my shoes gave out so I had to do the rest of the hike in my stocking feet. The mountain trail was straight up

When we got there we could hear the wailing and smell the woman's decomposing body. I'll never forget seeing her crushed head while village women sat near the corpse swatting flies.

As soon as we arrived, the tribe started the ceremony. The woman had been dead for three days. We watched the people wail, listen, cry and support each other. All of a sudden Roni was right beside me. He bent down, put his hand on a stump, and chopped off a finger with an ax. Right in front of me.

I jumped back and almost screamed. His finger lay on the stump. He was crying, less out of pain than for the loss of his mother. I didn't know what to do, even though I was the medic. It was important to us that we not intervene unless asked. Roni seemed fine. Nobody was freaking out by this. I noticed that many people there were missing a finger or two, but I attributed that to their working with machetes and axes. I didn't know that it was because they willingly cut them off to show their deep love for a person who has died. It was also a spiritual practice. The people in the tribe would put the cut-off stub of a finger in a banana leaf and hang it in the rafters to appease the spirits.

In the middle of the night I heard someone yelling, "Roni is dead! Roni is dead!" I tore out of the tent and I ran over to Roni. He lay bleeding on the ground, his hand in a bag, passed out. He was not dead.

I had never dealt with this kind of situation. What's more, I could see the bone where he had cut himself. I was scared, but I said to myself, "Take the fear with you. So what if you're scared, take it with you, do it anyway, he needs you." I acknowledged the fear, and then said, "Okay, come on, we're doing this." I cleaned up the stump and tied it off with a string, not knowing whether this was the proper procedure or not. I gave him antibiotics to prevent infection.

It was time to walk back and I still didn't have shoes. We hiked for eight more hours through the jungle and up and down the mountains. By the time we got to the last hill, I was green and had a burning fever.

I had food poisoning, from a Mumu, which is a type of oven that prepares food in the ground. I could barely move. I was violently shaking, and they had to push me up the last hill. I made it home, but I have never been sicker in my life. I thought I might die. I didn't have help. Joe didn't help with anything. I had that fear again, trying to take care of myself and Brayden. So I had to take the fear with me. That's what I learned from that experience and many others: you take the fear with you. You work through it, and you come out the other side. Otherwise, you let fear stop you.

If I had let fear stop me, Roni might have died. But he survived and he's fine. Whether it's life or death or not, take the fear with you. Everybody gets scared. Just do it anyway. It's worth it.

One of the tricks that I've learned to overcome fear is to visualize being on the other side. Visualize being safe and sound for whatever it is that you want to see happen.

With the helicopter adventure, I visualized us landing in the tribe and telling the story of how we had this crazy adventure of landing in the middle of the jungle, and along each step of the way, I didn't know what was going to happen, but I would visualize myself safe on the other side, telling the story. With the situation with Roni's finger, I visualized him happy and healthy and his finger perfectly healed up. Take the fear with you. Dance with it.

Steps and Methods

Here is how you can learn from my experiences.

Step 1. Keep your eye on the prize.

To start, ask yourself, "What do I want?"

When you are facing something that is scaring you, it's important that you focus on what it is that you want, not the fear. For me, it was getting home to our new village safely.

Ask yourself, "Why do I want this?" Write down all of the reasons that come to mind.

Commit to making it happen. Decide, make a choice, get strong — choose!

This step teaches you: don't let fear win.

Step 2. Take fear with you.

You can't wait for fear to leave to be okay or to move forward. Tell yourself right now, "I must move now, the only way is through." Repeat that until you believe it.

Talk to the fear, acknowledge him or her, and tell them there is nothing they can do to stop you, so either leave you alone or join the fun.

Take the leap. Take one small step at a time, and the next thing you know you will be experiencing what was once impossible. You are bigger than your fear! You've got this.

This step teaches you to use fear as fuel.

Step 3. Create your own mental movie.

See what you want to happen as if it's a movie playing in your mind. Visualize it going all your way!

Imagine how you would feel to overcome your fear and accomplish whatever it is that you want to see happen. The helicopter did come, we did get to land in our new home, and did we ever have an exciting story to tell!

Hear or smell whatever you experience. Write it down. For me, it was imagining hearing the helicopter come back over the mountains, to smell the fuel as it landed.

This step helps us understand that the mind is powerful — we need to use it!

When you follow and implement these steps, you will learn how to dance with fear, and how to focus on what you desire, not on what you fear. Here are the three steps so that you can do it, too:

- Keep your eye on the prize, on the goal.
- Take fear with you.
- Create your own mental movie.

The outcome in following these steps is that you will learn to not let fear win. The only way to handle fear is to go *straight through it!*

Intuition Is Seeing with the Soul

We can trust our intuition. We all have an inner compass that knows the way, if we will listen.

Here I will explore how best to hear your inner voice of direction. Once you hear your answer, act right away, don't get into analysis paralysis.

To illustrate this, I will share a story about intuiting the actions of my psychopathic ex-husband.

Then you will learn steps that will show you how you can listen and use your intuition to lead you:

1. Ask your higher self, "What do I need to hear or understand right now?"
2. Discover and use your formula for being able to hear your higher self/source.
3. Act now.

You will discover your intuition recipe. You will learn how to listen to your intuition and trust it so that you can follow it.

Your intuition is seeing with your soul. I've learned over the years that you can really trust it. It is there to guide you, in the best possible way, even when things don't make sense. Following it has always been the best thing. For me, one of the most prominent examples of hearing the voice of God/intuition was right before we ended up running to Mexico.

One morning, I woke up with the certainty that my abusive ex-husband Joe — who had been diagnosed by three different psychiatrists as a psychopath with a narcissistic personality disorder — was going to show up at my kids' school. There was no need for him to be there. He had never come to the school before in all the years since we left. He was an American, and his visitations, supervised by the Canadian government, were an hour or so away. He had never once asked about the kids' grades or anything to do with the school. I had worked at the school for years as a teacher's aide but was on medical leave due to a year and half of continuous migraines. I could barely function and spent most days in a dark room.

I had this feeling that morning that he would be coming to the school. I called our school secretary and told her that, even though it might sound crazy, that I had a feeling that my ex-husband would be coming and that she should be aware of this. I told her what he might say and do, but ultimately I felt that he was scoping out a way to kidnap the kids.

At 4:30 that afternoon, Tammy called, whispering, "He's here." My body and mind went into mama-bear mode and my nervous system went into fight or flight. I grabbed the kids and my husband Pete, and we ran and stayed in our trailer. We hid there for a couple weeks. Later, I found out from Tammy that Joe did exactly what I said he would do, almost word for word. Unfortunately the new school principal got charmed by him and didn't call the police as we had agreed. I got to the point where I decided that I couldn't live this way any more. My intuition was telling me, "It's time to do something drastic, you can't keep living like this. You have to do something."

I said to the boys, "Okay, let's go on vacation." We ended up on a plane to Mexico, and three days into being in Mexico my migraines went away, and I felt truly safe for the first time in my life. I thought, "Okay, we're gonna move to Mexico, and start over." And so we did. Within five weeks I had sold my house, and we were on our way to freedom.

There's a way to be able to tap into your intuition. My personal formula for listening to my intuition is by getting into a peak state by using the Diamond of Freedom, which I've spoken about before. By exercising or getting into nature, breathing, smiling and thinking about what I'm thankful for. And then I stop. I stop and meditate and connect to the Source and ask myself, "Okay, what do I need to know, understand or see, right now?" That's the question I ask: "What do I need to understand, know, or see right now?" Once you hear the answer, write it down.

And then ask again, "What else do I need to see? What else do I need to understand? What else do I need to know right now?" Write down your answer. Then act.

Don't wait to act, don't hem and haw. Don't get your brain into it with logic because that's going to be mostly fear. And sometimes things aren't logical.

For 12 years, nobody knew where we were. Mexico saved us, and we got to be free. Free from fear. Free from harassment. Free from the judgments and the guilt and the shame. We got to live our lives. And I can't even imagine what would have happened if I hadn't listened to that voice and if I hadn't taken action.

So listen to your intuition. Trust it. Take action. You won't always find out the reason, but often you will. Oftentimes you will find out why that was the answer and why that was what you needed to do. Like me, It could even save your life and the ones you love.

Steps and Methods

Here is how you can learn from my experience.

First center yourself and in the next chapter you will go over the Diamond of Freedom to get into a beautiful state.

Step 1. Ask your higher self, "What do I need to hear or understand right now?"

To start, stop whatever you're doing. Be present.

Set the intention of receiving guidance. Declare that you need help. Ask and you shall receive.

Ask yourself, "What do I need to see, hear, or understand right now?"

Write down whatever comes to mind. Don't worry about the how yet. Just listen for your answer. I did that when I sought to know what I should do to keep the boys safe. My answer was to move to Mexico and start over, and that I had to keep it a secret at all costs, that our lives depended on it.

Step 2. Discover and use your formula for being able to hear your higher self/Source in yourself.

It's important that you discover, if you don't already know, your success formula for listening to your higher self/intuition. Think about and create your own success formula for listening to your intuition.
For me, the first step is to get into nature. What is your first step? If you don't have one, ask yourself, "What should my first step be in my intuition formula?" Write down your answer. Maybe it's exercising, or taking a hot bath, or

listening to music.

Breathe. I usually breathe three times deeply. Breathe as long as you need to, to get to a state of peace and calmness. What is your second step? Write it down.

Practice gratitude. Make a list of things you're thankful for. Gratitude is the rocket ship to joy, so it's the fastest way to raise your frequency.

Listen. Ask yourself, "What do I need to see, hear or understand right now?"

If you have a different question that works better for you, then use that. Make sure you write it down. To listen, just sit quietly and listen to hear, listen to understand.

Step 3. Act now.

Receive the answer. It's not enough to just hear it. You also need to be open to actually receive it. Sometimes our need for certainty is so strong that we resist hearing that change might be what's necessary. So make sure you are open to hear what it is that you need to see, hear, or understand.

Trust the guidance that you're given.

When I got the answer to move, to leave everyone and everything I knew and move to Mexico, at first it was a shock. It was overwhelming, but I was also at peace because I knew it was the truth, I knew I had just been given the answer. I knew in my heart it was what I needed to do. So trust the guidance.

Take the first step forward.

My parents were the first people I told. I can see their faces clearly in my mind even now. They had a reaction of shock and then relief. They knew, too, that this is what we needed to do to stay safe! The next step was to put my house on the market. It sold in 15 minutes to the first people who looked at it.

Step by step. Do what you know to do. Period. It will all work out.

When you follow and implement these steps, you will learn that you can trust your intuition. You have an inner compass, a higher power within you, that knows the way if you will listen. You will know the importance of figuring out your intuition formula and how best to hear your inner voice of direction. You also have three steps on how you can listen and use your intuition to lead you:

1. Ask your higher self, "What do I need to hear or understand right now?"
2. Discover and use your own formula for being able to hear your higher self/source in you.
3. Act now.

You can learn how to listen to your intuition and trust it so you can follow it clearly and confidently.

In the next chapter, we'll explore breaking free from a programmed life.

 If you'd like further support from me, please use this QR. Looking forward to hearing from you!

Chapter 7

TRAINING YOUR ELEPHANT

In this chapter, I'm exploring how you don't have to live a programmed life. You can be yourself. You can train yourself to break free of the programming you've received.

You will learn that we have been running on autopilot most of our lives, but that we can make a choice — we don't have to be controlled by the program.

To illustrate this, I will share the story of how I discovered my elephant, and the need to train it. I learned to reprogram the way I run the majority of my time, and to become more aware of what I assign meaning to. I will also share with you the three steps to help you do the same:

1. There are two minds: the subconscious and the conscious.
2. The body gets accustomed to following the mind. Autopilot.
3. Make your choice on what you assign meaning to.

It's amazing to move from the subconscious to the conscious mind, to make a choice that serves you!

Did you know you have an elephant to train? I didn't know that, either, until all of a sudden I did. And this is when I realized that there are two minds, the subconscious mind, and the conscious mind.

Guess which is the biggest? That's right, the subconscious mind takes up 95% of our mind. Only five percent of our mind is conscious. This basically means that we are 95% zombie, running on whatever program that has been pressed upon us via our culture, our parents, our environment, our schools, our friends.

Training Your Elephant

I got the elephant idea when I saw a picture of a boy riding an elephant. The boy was so much smaller than the elephant that the idea of the 95% and the 5% came into my mind. I had the thought that we need to train this elephant of ours. That we need to tell our subconscious what to do or else it — the elephant — is going to run us. When you realize that you have an elephant, you'll also realize that your elephant has not been trained. You didn't even know until this moment that you had one, let alone needed to train him.

So he's a rogue elephant. For example, when someone cuts you off in traffic, you get angry. The elephant knows that you always get angry. So now you have to train him to act differently.

Your brain's going to have fits. Do you notice your brain having fits when you try to change things? That's your elephant. So you have to train and love your elephant. You've got to love them, not beat him/her, but you also have to tell them where to go and what to do. Otherwise, it's going to run on the program that it's been running on up until this point.

I had a program that ran in my subconscious that said I need to be busy all the time, or else I was lazy. I created this stressed, crazy-busy existence. I used to tell people how busy I was all the time because I thought that being busy was the best, and it gave me significance and made me feel good. When you realize that you don't have to think that way, you get to do it differently.

It's important that we create the meanings we want that serve us best. One day I got help on this from my mentor, Josh. I had been having nightmares every night for probably 10 years. I had continued to feel unsafe, living in fear after fleeing to Mexico to keep my kids safe from my abusive ex-husband. Josh looked at me and said, "You're safe. You don't need to live like you're in danger anymore. You're safe."

I looked at him with tears in my eyes. "But how do you know for sure?"

"You're safe," he said. "Safety is whatever you decide to be in the moment. Right now, you're safe. Nothing is happening. So right now, you're safe, so be safe. Live. Let the stress go. Change the meaning, change the dialogue that you're not safe because it's not true — you are, you're safe. Look at you right here in front of me. Safe."

A light bulb came on in my mind, and my whole body relaxed. And the nightmares quit.

With that realization, I was able to release that internal fear and things changed. My elephant was able to relax, and didn't need to be on the defense and the offensive all at the same time. Change the meaning that you put to things. Change your life.

Next time someone suddenly pulls in front of you in traffic, you don't have to get angry because maybe the new meaning is, "Oh, he must not have seen me. I do that sometimes, too." And you don't go through even a blip of anger. It all depends on what we put meaning to, so let's create meaning that serves us best.

Steps and Methods

Here's how you can learn from my experience.

Center yourself and breathe. Ask your higher self for truth and clarity.

Step 1. There are two minds — the subconscious and the conscious. The subconscious runs the show, and it's programming from childhood.

To start, picture yourself riding an elephant. Ask yourself, "How has my un-trained elephant affected me in the past?" Write down anything that comes to mind without judgment.

Know that there are two minds: the conscious makes up 5%, the subconscious 95%. This helped me have grace for myself and for others.

Wake up. Don't go back to sleep. You will be tempted to, because sometimes it's easier not to know. We can continue on as zombies and blame everyone and everything for what our elephant is doing. Don't be like the masses. Be different.

It's important that you can see the elephant as separate from yourself, but you are still responsible to guide and love them in the way they should go. Take a minute to become acquainted with your elephant.

Step 2. The body gets accustomed to following the mind.

Realize that you have been on autopilot for as many years as you have been alive. This really helped me understand some of my choices and behaviors over the years. I had an elephant running the show, or in other words, a program that was controlling me. I've trained my elephant in making choices, and the shift has been tremendous. I am the leader much of the time now. I am a zombie much less frequently.

What we think and what we attach meaning to creates emotions, and emotions are our life. Let us be aware of what meaning we are putting on things, because changing the meaning equals changing your response. Change your life.

It all depends on what meaning you attach to it. Choose what you want to have meaning — but be careful what you attach meaning to.

Make sure you attach a meaning that helps you, inspires you, serves you. You have a choice. You don't have to be merely reactive (letting the elephant programming run wild). You can choose what you put meaning to and therefore control how you feel about something.

Step 3. Make Your Choice

Ask yourself, "What am I thinking?" and "What am I attaching meaning to?" Write down anything that comes to mind. I had created the meaning that I had to be busy or else I was lazy. Change the meaning, change your life. Now I congratulate myself for resting and being balanced.

Ask yourself, "Is it serving me?" Yes or no. If it is, keep it; if it isn't, change it. Boom. Is what you are attaching meaning to, serving you?

Ask yourself, "What would serve me?" Write down anything that comes to mind. Keep asking until you have a couple examples. Pick the one that makes you feel the most happy or empowered. What is your new empowered meaning?

Learn how to move from the subconscious to the conscious mind to make a choice that serves you.

If you follow these steps, you will start to get control of your emotions. You will learn that we have been running on autopilot most of our lives, but that we can make a choice. We don't have to be controlled by the program. You will learn to be aware of what meaning you are putting on things because: change the meaning, change your response, change your life. You now have three steps to help you get control of your elephant:

- Realize & accept that you have two minds: subconscious & conscious.
- Your body is used to following your mind. So you're mostly on autopilot
- Get into the habit of consciously choosing what meanings you assign.

You need to become aware of what meanings you are assigning, and the emotions that follow. You will have the skill of how to wake yourself up from the zombie state that you are in most of the time, long enough to make choices for yourself. Train your elephant! Take back your life!

There Are Only Two States of Being

HAPPY	CRAPPY
EXCITED	ANGRY
JOY	SAD
HAPPY	JEALOUS
PEACE	TIRED
CONTENT	LONELY
CALM	PISSED OFF
THANKFUL	STRESSED
PASSION	WORRIED
ELATED	FEARFUL

Are you crappy or happy? Those are really the only two states of being. Or in other words you are either suffering, or not suffering. A beautiful state is the absence of suffering.

Here, I will share with you how easy it is to know what state you are in and the importance of celebrating when you become aware of where you are.

Happiness is not something that happens to us: it's a choice. To illustrate this,

I'll relate a story about getting a scorpion sting. I will then give you the steps on how to choose your state of being:

1. Realize the state you are in.
2. Celebrate that you just woke up.
3. Choose to be happy.

You will learn that there are only two states of being: crappy or happy, and that it's super easy to figure out which one you are in. Once you know, you can do something about it!

We're either crappy or happy. You can't be on the fence. It's pretty evident if you're in a crappy mood, and it's pretty evident if you're in a happy mood. There are levels to happiness, and there are levels to crappiness, but it's really not hard to tell which one you are in. So the beautiful thing is that there's only two, so it's easy.

One day when getting ready for work, I went into my closet to pull out a dress, and I suddenly felt as if I'd been jammed with a needle through my middle finger. My brain was trying to make sense of it. I looked at my finger, but couldn't see anything. The pain was enormous. I was confused.

Then I saw a small blond scorpion scurrying away to hide elsewhere among my things. I couldn't even get to him. I quickly went to the sink and ran my finger underwater, but the pain was intense.

I didn't know what to do. I called Brett, a coworker, and said, "Dude, I just got stung by a scorpion."

Brett asked, "What color was it?"

"It was one of those blond ones."

"Oh, no, those are the bad ones," he said "You need to go to the hospital."

I drove to the hospital holding the steering wheel with my elbows while keeping my finger raised. It looked like I was flipping everyone off as I drove. I realized that I had a choice. I could be in a crappy mood or I could be happy. I literally howled my way to the hospital, both in pain and in total enjoyment of a moment that I decided to consider "freaking funny."

There I was, giving everyone the bird as I was driving. People didn't know it was because of a scorpion sting, and I had a big smile on my face. When I got to the hospital, I'm in a great state. In terrible pain, but in a great state anyway.

The doctor told me, "It's going to hurt like hell for a few hours, but you'll be fine."

The point of this is that I actually had a wonderful time in the midst of a horrible time, or what could have been a horrible time. It really wasn't that bad a time. I was in a lot of pain, but I was okay because I had changed my state of mind. So I celebrated that and gave myself a virtual high five.

Celebrate your progress. Give yourself a pat on the back. Do anything that you can do to acknowledge the moment that you realize that you're in a crappy state, because in that glorious, glorious moment, you have the chance to choose.

In that glorious moment, you are no longer a zombie. You're no longer the elephant. You are the human riding your elephant, and you're in charge. Celebrate it and then change it.

Steps and Methods

Here is how you can learn from my experience.

Step 1. Realize the state you are in.

To start, take a second to stop. Stop whatever you are doing or thinking. Take a second to be present.

The second step is breathing. Breathe deeply into your lungs through your nose, hold for five seconds, and exhale through your mouth, making the sound "ahh" (as you do before each of these steps). Exhale for as long as you can to release any stale air. The ahh sound helps release stress. Do this three times. I do this often throughout the day, now. It's amazing! It helps my stress levels so much! So breathe!

Ask yourself, "What state am I in? Am I crappy or happy?" Breathe and choose. After I got stung by a scorpion, I decided not to be a victim, but to be happy regardless.

Step 2. Celebrate that you just woke up.

As soon as you realize you are in a happy mood or even a crappy mood, celebrate! Do something to acknowledge the fact that you just woke the hell up. Why do we celebrate? It's to reprogram our minds to not condemn ourselves and think we are less than, like we normally do when we realize we are messing up. So celebrate not being a zombie for that moment!

Step 3. Choose to be happy. Realize you have a choice to continue to suffer or not. You no longer have to be miserable.

Your circumstances don't have to dictate how you feel.

Ask yourself, "Where in my life am I choosing to suffer?" Write down anything that comes to mind without judgment. Come up with at least two or three examples.

With each item on the list you just wrote, ask yourself, "Moving forward, am I going to choose crappy or happy?" Continue down your list and ask the question above again and again until you have completed your list.

Knowing that you can decide how to feel helps you become aware of the consequences and the emotions that follow.

When you follow and implement these steps you will understand that crappy or happy are really the only two states of being. You will learn that you can choose happiness, just like in the story about my scorpion sting and how I was able to laugh even though I was in so much pain. You have the steps on how to choose your state:

- Realize the state you are in.
- Celebrate that you just woke up.
- Choose to be happy.

When you wake up to the state that you are in, you realize and see yourself apart from that state. Celebrating waking up will reprogram the brain to want to wake up more. The truth is that we decide how we feel, and the natural consequences and emotions follow. You will learn that it's super easy to figure out if you're in a crappy or happy state. And you can do something about it. Choose to be happy!

Don't Be a Diamond in the Rough, Be a Diamond!

It's time to take back control and shine!

Here, I want to explore why changing your physiology is the easiest first step to changing how we feel. You can do that by asking just one question that can help you turn everything around and feel differently. It's important to realize that we have stories that run over and over like a broken record that tell us bullshit and we believe it. We have to stop the repeating record and replace it with a new one.

We can connect to our higher selves, to Source, anytime we want. To illustrate this, I will share with you the story of how I missed a flight to the Philippines. I will also share an example of gratitude in the story with my dad in the hospital thanking his doctors.

In addition, you will have four steps to change your state:

1. Physiology: smile, breathe, move.
2. Focus: what are you thankful for?
3. Story: realize what you tell yourself may be false — replace it with what is true.
4. Connect to Source: remember, we are one.

You will learn the steps to happiness and how to be in control of your emotions and therefore your life!

Changing your physiology is amazing because it changes how you feel so fast. I do it constantly, now. One of the times I practiced this was when the kids and I flew the red-eye to the Philippines. When we arrived, we had missed our flight from Manila to the island of Cebu. So there we were, three teenagers and I. We were trashed. We hadn't slept, it was a long, long flight, and then we found out we'd totally missed our flight to get to Cebu.

So what did I do? I smiled, and I took a few deep breaths. I moved my body and I shook off the day and I shook off the night, and I said, "OK, let's figure this out."

With a big smile on my face, I walked into the ticket office. Literally 15 minutes later, I had four new flights to the island of Cebu, and we didn't even have to stay overnight. We were able to leave a couple hours later, so it all worked out. I wonder how different that interaction could have been if I hadn't done those four things, if I hadn't smiled, breathed, moved, changed my focus and my story, and connected to Source. I might have walked into that office in a completely different state, a grumpy state, an angry state. And who knows if they would have found me a flight, or if it would have gone so smoothly?

I practice what I call the Diamond of Freedom. The Diamond of Freedom is a four-step process of getting your shit together and changing your state. It gives you freedom from suffering, freedom from feeling stuck, angry, helpless, etc. and creates freedom to live, to love, to enjoy, to be truly happy.

The first step is to change the position of your body by smiling, breathing and moving it. The second point is to change what you are focused on and ask yourself, "What am I thankful for?" The third step is to replace the bullshit you are telling yourself. And the fourth point of the diamond is to connect to Source and know you are not alone and ask for divine help.

One of the best examples I have of the second part of the diamond, (focus - what you're focused on, what are you thankful for) is with my father, when he found out that he needed to have open heart surgery, a quadruple bypass.

I flew up to Canada to be with my mom and dad during that time. And man, I had to work the diamond a lot. And he did, too, in his own way. He was on the operating table, and they were just about to put him under when he stopped them and said, "Wait a second, wait, hold on a second." The operating room staff were taken aback. I don't think many people do that. My dad said, "I just want you to know, and I just want to thank you in advance for what you are going to do for me today."

And they smiled. And he said, "I'm so thankful for the sex change that you're going to give me. This is a big day." And they all went, "What?" and with a ginormous smile my dad said, "Just kidding! I know I'm here for my heart." And they all burst out laughing. It broke their state, and it helped foster camaraderie among the doctors and nurses. My dad was no longer just a body on an operating table. He was a person.

Then my dad said, "Seriously, I really want to thank you in advance for what you're doing for me, because you're not just doing this for me. You are doing this for my wife, my three kids, and my five grandkids. My family and I just want to thank you in advance for how you're going to help me, and I'm so thankful for all the years of service, for all the years of school, to get you to the point of being able to help me in this way today."

He told me this story after he came out of surgery. What he said just blew them away. Dad had gratitude going into open heart surgery. And I have no doubt that he made those doctors love him. He came out with flying colors and he recovered so fast, the doctors were shocked at how well he was doing. Gratitude is a beautiful and powerful thing.

We have to watch what we say to ourselves and what we say to others. Self-dialogue can be damaging. Especially when we say such things to ourselves as, "I'm not good enough. I can't be loved. Life is hard." They're just not true. The major limiting belief that I had growing up was "life is hard." I had heard this from my family probably thousands of times.

They also believed life was amazing. But I heard over and over again that life was hard. So guess what happens when you start believing something like that, that life is hard? You start looking for reasons to make that true. And so I'm like, yup, see, there it is. Life is hard. Yep. See, there it is again. Life is hard. I find myself in a shitty marriage. Life is hard. It's the way it is, right? And I settled and stayed for eight years, at least in part because life is hard. When I realized that that was my belief system, not me, I had to annihilate it. I said to myself, "No way am I going to let this rule my life, choices, or decisions from this day forward."

So I replaced it with what's true. And when you do that, you get it into your cells. You have to tell your elephant what to do. You've got to tell him with conviction. He's got to believe you. The truth is that life is amazing. Life is magical. Life is full of purpose. Life is full of connections. Life is full of opportunities. Life is full of adventure. Life is full of love. That's what life is.

When you say it with conviction and with some volume, guess what? Your elephant's going to go, "Huh? She seems serious. Maybe this is true." And then the next time you hear the words in your mind, "Life is hard," you're like, "No, that's bullshit. What's true is..." and you say it again, "Life is amazing. Life is magical. Life is full of purpose. Life is full of opportunities. Life is full of adventure. Life is epic. That's what's true."

Then, pretty soon, your elephant is going to start believing you and you're going to start looking for the magic, and looking for the opportunities, and looking for the connections, and looking for the love. And it changes your life.

We can't forget about the fourth step, which could also be the first step, but for us in our humanness, sometimes we have to go around the diamond and get to the fourth step last.

But if you're able to do the fourth step first, please do that, and that is to connect to Source, to connect to God, to understand there is a higher power in and around and everywhere that is seeking to help us, that is seeking to encourage us, that is seeking to listen. Remember you are tapped into the quantum field, the universal intelligence.

I did that while sitting in the waiting room while my dad was in surgery. I just really connected to God and just prayed and gave my dad to the Divine, to Source. I was able to go through that waiting room with very little stress and worry because of these tips and tools that I have in the shape of this glorious diamond.

Diamond of Freedom

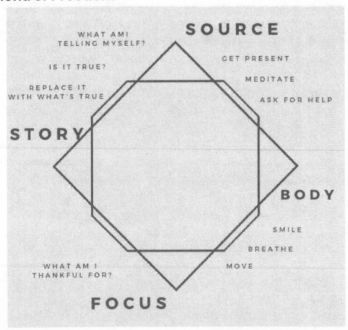

The diamond teaches us how to handle life. How to handle it in such a way that you get immense joy out of it instead of being miserable and suffering. Suffering does not have to be the way. It does not have to be normal. We have a choice. We always have a choice. Source is always right there, whether we remember or not, whether we acknowledge or not, the divine is there and we can tap in and we can receive so much strength and so much love and so much wisdom when we take a minute to connect.

Steps and Methods

Here is how I go from crappy to happy and how I work the Diamond of Freedom.

Step 1. Physiology — smile, breathe, move.

To start, smile. On a scale of 1-10, how do you feel right now? Take inventory of yourself and write down a number. When you realize you are in a crappy mood or you want to prepare yourself to be in an even better mood, you work the first point of the diamond. Physiology is the first thing you do to change your state of being, and therefore how you feel. In other words, change what you are doing in your body. Change your physiology. Emotions have a look. Think about someone who is depressed, their shoulders will be slumped, head down, frown on their face, right? Excitement has a look. Emotions have a look. Change your body, change your emotions.

Then breathe. We normally breathe shallowly. Pretend you are filling your lungs from the bottom up. If you do it correctly, your stomach will expand, and your shoulders won't move up. Breathe deep into the lungs again. Make sure it's through your nose, hold for five seconds, and exhale through your mouth making the sound "ahh." The "ahh" sound helps release stress. I do it a lot in my car when I'm driving, as there is usually no one else in the car, and I can be as weird as I want.

Next, move your ass! Walk, dance, bike, jump around, exercise, or run, just to name a few you can do, but you have to move. When you feel shitty, the worst thing you can do is stay in the slumped position you are in.

Step 2. Focus on what you are thankful for.

"Where your focus goes, energy flows." This is a Tony Robbins quote. What you focus on matters. If you feel shitty, you have shitty thoughts. Period. So it's important for you to control what you are focused on.

Ask yourself, "What am I thankful for?" Here's the thing: it won't matter what your elephant was thinking about before, as soon as you ask that question he will be looking for an answer.

You can't be scared or angry in the presence of gratitude. So get thankful. Train yourself to ask this question over and over all day long.

Step 3. Be aware of the stories you tell yourself. Replace them with what's true.

Ask yourself, "What am I telling myself?"

The third point of the diamond is your language, your verbiage, or your story. What record are you playing over and over again? Is it, "I'm not good enough, I'm too fat, too skinny, too slow, too fast, too educated, not educated enough, etc.?" Ask yourself what you're telling yourself now. Become aware of your own self-talk.

Ask yourself, "Is this true?" It's likely that you're telling yourself nothing but bullshit. So say this: "No, it's bullshit." Say it with certainty, or your elephant won't pay attention. Replace it with what's true.

Step 4. Connect to the Source, remembering we are one with it.

Be quiet for a minute. I usually stop whatever I'm doing for a minute and be silent. I put my intention and my attention on connecting to Source. Remember: Where my attention is, is where I place my energy. So place your energy/attention on the Source.

When you follow and implement these steps, you will take back control of your life and shine! You will understand that changing your physiology is the easiest first step to changing how we feel.

We have stories that we constantly tell ourselves that are bullshit that we believe, so we need to replace them with new, empowered beliefs. We also need to remember how important it is that we can connect to our higher selves. Using the Diamond, you have the four steps on how to control your state:

- Physiology: smile, breathe, move.
- Focus: what you're thankful for.
- Story: realize what bullshit you are telling yourself and replace that with what is true.

- Connect to Source: remember that we are one.

We don't have to believe our own bullshit — we can change the story and remember that we always have the divine with us at all times, that we don't have to go through life alone.

What about Violence, Abuse, Rape, Death?

Will I be able to move on from the big traumas in life? Can I be okay even in the middle of a major trauma?

In this section, I share how to take yourself from freaked-out to fine. Now you can wake up from the zombie programming, and separate yourself from it so you can make a conscious choice and also give yourself the chance to lose your unwanted bullshit programming in a controlled way, if you need to.

To illustrate this, I will share with you the story of when my best friend Dani was stabbed. Then you will learn three steps for getting through a trauma:

1. Realize the trauma.
2. Work the Diamond.
3. Two minutes of suffering; keep working the Diamond.

You will become more conscious of what's going on, and realize that even in the toughest situations you can be okay, and you won't store stress and trauma within your body. You will learn how no matter what is going on in your life this four-step process can get you through it.

My best friend Daniela (Dani) was stabbed nine times during a robbery. Somehow she was able to call me. I was in a meeting, and my mind couldn't compute as she said, in a weak voice, "I've been stabbed." Suddenly I got it, and burst into action. "I'm on my way, stay with me on the phone," I said. As it happened I was standing outside the best hospital in town. I ran into the lobby and handed the phone to an attendant there to get Dani's address correct. Then I ran back into my car and the ambulance and I tore to her house. On the way, I discovered her attacker had left. Her daughter Sophia, who was in the house at the time, was untouched.

I stayed on the phone with Dani. I knew to keep speaking with her to keep her conscious. I reminded her to put pressure on the wound, assuming she had been stabbed once. She told me that she couldn't; she didn't have the strength because she had been stabbed so many times. With those words, the blood drained out of my face. I started working the diamond. I kept breathing deeply and getting her to breathe as well. I kept telling myself she would be okay, and I was calling on Source to please save her.

At one point, she said she felt cold. I knew this was a bad sign. I had her visualize a beautiful hot tub of super perfect warm water cascading around her, and I told her I was almost there. I screeched to a halt outside her door right behind the ambulance. I walked in and there she was, lying on the kitchen floor, blood everywhere, people everywhere.

I jumped around the puddles of blood to be at her head. I looked into her terrified eyes and told her she was going to be okay. Help was here. The paramedics bandaged her up the best they could, but they didn't even know at the time how many times she had been stabbed. They asked which hospital they should take her to. I looked into their eyes and said to the very best one. There was a bit of a debate because there was a different hospital closer. I intuitively knew that to save her, it would require the best doctors and equipment!

Luckily, I had trained her on the Diamond. I encouraged her. I said, "Honey, you're gonna do great, you're gonna be a bright, shining light of how NOT to be a victim."

When we got to the hospital and she was safely in the doctors' capable hands, I allowed myself to lose my shit, and I gave myself two minutes to cry my eyes out. Then I did what I needed to do to be the friend that she needed at that moment.

She died twice on the table. They took one kidney and her spleen. Her kidney was completely obliterated from being stabbed so many times. Dani told me the attacker walked her across the living room with the knife inside her as he repeatedly stabbed her with the knife using the same hole. So there was no way to save the kidney. The next day, her vitals were completely stable. It was a miracle!

You should have seen the doctors' faces — they could not believe it! She would have to be in the hospital from a month to two months, they said. Guess how many days she actually stayed in the hospital? One week! How? Because she controlled her state. She worked the Diamond of Freedom over and over until she left that hospital one week later.

She continues to work the Diamond to control her state, and she is a bright shiny example of how not to be a victim. The forensic doctor at the trial said these words and I'll never forget them: "There's only one reason Dani is alive, and that's because she willed herself to be so!" So, yes, working the Diamond helps with even the really big stuff that happens in our lives.

Steps and Methods

Here is how you can learn from me:

Step 1. Realize the trauma.

To start, wake up. When you find yourself in a traumatic situation, the best way to keep you from freaking out is to realize that you are starting to freak out. When Dani told me she had been stabbed so many times, I realized I had a choice.

Celebrate that you woke up. Acknowledge that you just jumped off the moving train. That alone will help you stay off. Being able to see yourself separate from the program of freak out will make the difference in how you handle the crisis.

Make your choice. Choose whether you will freak out or you'll be okay. You can choose to be okay. So make your choice.

Step 2. Work the Diamond of Freedom

Breathe, smile, move. As soon as I became awake and aware while flying down the road to Dani, I started working the Diamond by breathing. That changed how I felt.

Ask, "What am I thankful for?" In those moments of that situation, I was thankful for ambulances, doctors, nurses, and that I could be there for Dani. I was thankful for hospitals, and medicines.

The second step in working the diamond is becoming aware of what you are focusing on. I could have thought how likely it was that she might die, or I could ask what I was grateful for. Which question do you think serves you the best? Exactly! Gratitude is the answer.

Ask, "What am I telling myself?" The third point of the Diamond is your language, or self talk. So I started being conscious of what I was telling myself. I told myself that she would be okay and that she would get the help she needed in time. And that's what happened.

Remind yourself who you are and who lives in you. I remembered who lives in me and who I can call on at any time, and so I prayed for help, for guidance.

Step 3. Two minutes of suffering, keep working the Diamond.

When you are going through any difficult or traumatic situation, it's important that you let it out. The first step is to realize that you are having a hard time.

Let yourself cry or yell to release it. It's important to release it. I give myself two minutes of suffering.

Go back to working the Diamond and doing/being whatever or whoever you need to be. Smile, breathe, move, think about what you are thankful for, tell yourself the positive truth (you've got this) and pray for guidance. Period.

When you follow and implement these steps, you will have the skills to help yourself in even the big traumas in life. You will KNOW how to take yourself from freaked out to fine. You will KNOW HOW to wake up from the program, and separate yourself from it so that you can make a conscious choice. And to also give yourself the chance to lose your shit in a controlled way, if you need to — just like Dani did in being stabbed and willing herself to live. The three steps on how to get through a trauma are

- Realize the trauma,
- Work the diamond,
- Two minutes of suffering; keep working the Diamond.

No matter what is going on in your life this four-step process can get you through it.

In the next chapter, we will explore how you can take responsibility for your life.

 If you'd like further support from me, please use this QR. Looking forward to hearing from you!

Chapter 8

WAKE UP! TAKE RESPONSIBILITY FOR YOUR LIFE!

We are all programmed, and we conduct our lives according to certain things that have been programmed into our psyches, things we learn from family, school, society, friends.

In this chapter, I explore how you can change the programming and replace it with a way of life that serves you best. You can examine your presuppositions, your perspectives, and your personal prejudices to look at what makes you do what you do, and think as you think. As you free yourself from pre-existing points of view, you will be able to become freer and, in the end, happier.

Here, I will explore how you can yank out the programming that says "Thou shalt suffer," and replace it with things that serve you best. I will share with you the story of the Hot Cup of Coffee experiment. I will also give you steps on how to take back control of your mind and your life:

1. Realize that we are constantly getting programmed.
2. Protect yourself.
3. Choose what you want to believe after researching thoroughly.

The outcome is to realize you are being programmed and the importance of taking action to protect your mind, and to learn to research and seek to understand, and not just take everything at face value. You will learn how to wake up from the zombie state and become a human being with choices. You will learn how not to be a sheeple.

Our Programming

We have been programmed since the moment we were born: from our culture and our families, parents, siblings, friends, schools, sports clubs, anybody we have access to. Most of this is subconscious, because, remember, we're 95% subconscious. And so we don't even realize that we are being programmed.

In October 2008, Yale University published a study featuring "hot coffee or iced coffee." To test a hypothesis about the importance of temperature, research assistants casually tested the undergraduate test subjects by having them briefly hold either a warm cup of coffee or iced coffee as they wrote down information. The subjects were then given a packet of information about an individual and then asked to assess his or her personality traits. The participants assessed the person as significantly "warmer" if they had previously held the warm cup of coffee rather than the iced cup of coffee.

In the second study, participants held therapeutic packs that were heated or frozen and were then told they could receive a gift certificate for a friend or a gift for themselves. Those who held the hot pack were more likely to ask for the gift certificate, while those who held the frozen pack tended to keep the gift.

So imagine what is literally being programmed into our life directly. We have to pay attention, and we need to stand guard at the door of our minds. It is 95% programming. (It's probably higher than that, but I just don't want to be extreme.) I am not going to be told what to think. I want to engage in my own thinking.

The mainstream media is a massive programmer of fear. Some think that if you get rid of news, that you're not going to know what's going on, but it's not true. There's so many other ways to get information out there that aren't from the national news. You can research in a more conscious way, see the truth from other angles, and you can look at different sources, so that you can get a big picture idea of what's going on instead of one angle with a specific purpose to get you to believe whatever it is that they want you to believe.

Steps and Methods

Here is how you can learn from my experience.

Center yourself and breathe. Work the Diamond of Freedom. Breathe, move, think about what you are thankful for, tell yourself the truth, connect to Source!

Step 1. Realize that we are constantly getting programmed

To start, realize that your thoughts are not fully your own thoughts. Sometimes a hot cup of coffee influences how you think and feel about something. Taking a minute to understand this will help you as you navigate situations in the future. Becoming aware of what we are thinking and feeling is key. What thoughts and feelings have you taken on that are not really yours?

Ask yourself, "What information is feeding my mind?" News? Friends? Church? Communities? Think about anything that is outside of you that is beneficial or not beneficial. Write it all down.

Step 2. Protect yourself

Ask yourself, "Out of all the outside information that I take in on a consistent basis, which ones aren't serving me well?" Write down what you come up with.

Ask yourself, "What outside information should I eliminate altogether, and what should I reduce?"

Write down anything that comes to mind. Then take action, make some decisions, and follow through on them.

You can give it a 30-day experiment, as you can make a change for almost anything if you know it's just for 30 days. If you think it's forever, it can become too much to handle and you quit. So try it for 30 days. Here's what's great about it — you will KNOW the benefits within that time. Then you can decide if you want to keep going or not.

Remember that it's important to not just tell your brain/elephant "No" — you must replace whatever you remove with something else, or it will just go back to the old ways. Write down anything that comes to mind. The outcome of this step is to take action to protect your mind.

Step 3. Choose what you want to believe after researching well.

Ask yourself, "What is something I have been told/programmed to believe that doesn't feel quite right?" Write down anything that comes to mind, without judgment.

Ask your higher self, "What is the truth?" Write down anything that comes to mind.

This step helps you learn to research and seek to understand, not to take everything at face value.

When you follow and implement these steps, you will understand that you don't have to be a zombie, but that you are a real live person with choices.

You now have the steps on how to take back control of your mind:

- Realize that we are constantly getting programmed.
- Protect yourself.
- Choose what you want to believe after researching thoroughly.

You will learn how to wake up from the zombie state and become a human being with choices. You will learn learn how not to be a controlled sheeple.

Victim or Victor: Which Are You?

Life is happening *for* you, not *to* you. But we are programmed to feel victimized; it's our go-to thought. Unless you replace the old thought with a new one, the old one is going to keep on playing.

Here are the steps to create a new, empowering philosophy:

1. Become aware of my mind, which tells me that I'm a victim.
2. Replace that programming with a new belief that "Life is happening for me."
3. Believe it. Trust it.

For many of us, our first thought in certain situations is "Poor me." But you can change your thinking from victim to victor! It's important to trust the new philosophy which, when adopted, will transform your life for the better. Imagine not spending your life as a victim anymore, but instead living like the victor that you are!

What separates the victim from the victor? Perspective. One of the most unbelievable examples I share is being in the ambulance on the way to the hospital with my friend Dani after she was stabbed. I was terrified for her. I lifted her head underneath my hands and I held her head as we flew down the highway, siren blaring. I looked down into her big, brown, puppy-dog eyes and I can see how scared she is and this overwhelming wave of fear passed over me. I wanted to puke. I wanted to cry. I wanted to collapse. The fear was that I was going to lose my best friend. Then I remembered my training. I remembered the phrase that I learned from my mentor, Tony Robbins: "Life is happening *for* you. Not *to* you." I had this other realization: if life is happening for me and I'm not more special than anybody else on the planet, then that means life is also happening *for* Dani, and she just got stabbed *nine* times.

And so I was able in that moment of realization to look down at her and say, "You've got this, girl. Everything is working out. Look, you're in an ambulance. You are not alone on the floor. We are in an ambulance. We are getting help. They know what they're doing. There's a hospital that we can actually go to. Every cell in your body right now is working for you. It is clotting the blood. It is keeping you from bleeding out. You are healing right now. Here's what we're going to do. When you get through this, we're going to do so many amazing things, and we're going to *travel!*"

Then I asked her, "Where do you want to go? New York?" She nodded. I said, "Okay, let's go to New York. We'll go to New York, and we'll see snow." She had never seen snow, and I knew she really wanted to, and we could see the lights at Christmas. "And we're going to have that experience together someday. And Sophie, you're going to see Sophia grow up." Sophia is her daughter. "Sophia needs you." I prayed to the divine for help and kept encouraging her the best I could.

I was able to do that because my philosophy is that life is happening *for* me and not *to* me.

When you're looking for the gifts, guess what? You find them. The negative is available to you at any time, and so is the positive. Both are available to you. I was able to be the friend that Dani needed me to be at that moment, because I remembered that life is happening *for* us, not *to* us. And Dani now knows this, too, and she lives that. Will you?

Steps and Methods

Here is how you can learn from my experience.

Step 1. Become aware of my mind, which tells me I'm a victim.

To start, wake up to the existence of the repeated thought of "poor me."

In order not to be a victim, we have to first wake up to the fact that we think that we are. As soon as you hear yourself say "poor me," give yourself a pat on the back, because you just woke up! You just became separate from the program and can now see yourself. For me, it was on the ambulance ride. So ask yourself where you're being a victim. Write down anything that comes to mind.

Work the Diamond. Remember the Diamond of Freedom is a four-step process of getting your shit together and changing your state.

The first step is to change the position of your body by smiling, breathing, and moving it.

The second point is to change what you are focused on and ask yourself, "What am I thankful for?"

The third step is to replace the bullshit you are telling yourself, like in this instance, "Dani is going to die" to "Dani's going to come out of this with flying colors."

And the fourth point of the Diamond is to connect to Source and know you are not alone and ask for divine help. Right now I want you to go through the steps of working the Diamond in preparation for the exercise that follows.

Choose a new thought. In other words, choose a new philosophy. Would you agree that the "poor me" thinking does not ultimately serve you? I encourage you to adopt the one that I now have: life is happening *for* me, not *to* me. I suggest you write it down and place it all over your house and car.

Step 2. Replace it with the new belief that "life is happening for me, and everything is here to help me."

Ask yourself, "What is true here and now?" In order to change your mind and train your elephant, you must replace the old, established thought with a new one. You can snap yourself out of it, by asking what's true in the here and now. The here and now are what matter.

Ask yourself, "What do you want to be true in the future?" Believe that. See that. Describe in detail to yourself or others what it is that you would like to see happen.

Tell yourself, "Life is happening *for* me, not *to* me!" I'm stressing this point a lot because this philosophy alone will completely transform your life. The ripple effect will be epic. Life is happening *for* you, *and* everything is here to help you!

This step provides a chance to change your thinking from victim to victor!

Step 3. Believe it. Trust it.

Choose to trust it. The alternative is misery.

Make a conscious choice right now to trust me, to trust it. If you don't, then tomorrow you will likely go right back to the belief that the world is out to get you, and that means misery.

The second step is to trust this new philosophy, and to see and visualize great things happening in the moment and things to come. So practice that right now. Life is happening *for* you, and everything is here to help you.

This step helps you trust the new philosophy.

When you follow and implement these steps, you will have a new understanding that life is happening *for* you, not *to* you. You will know the importance of replacing the old thought with the new one.

To recap, I shared steps to creating a new empowering philosophy:

1. Become aware of your mind as it tells you that you are a victim.
2. Replace that negative thought with a new belief that "Life is happening *for* me."
3. Believe it. Trust it.

You can change your thinking from victim to victor.

In Everything There Is a Gift

What if there were a gift in everything?

Here, you'll learn that even though shit does sometimes hit the fan, you can find a gift in every situation. Life can be a whole lot of fun when you look for gifts everywhere.

To illustrate this, I'll share a story of missing a flight. And then you will have a few steps to help you look on the bright side:

1. Become aware that shit is hitting the fan.

2. Literally look around you for the gift in it.
3. Go with the flow of knowing and enjoying the constant gifts, and be grateful.

You will wake up to the situation so that you can separate yourself from it to be able to control your thoughts. You know that only then can you take the time to look for the gifts, and that they are everywhere. Enjoy the magic that exists all around you! From following and implementing these steps you will learn how to look at life through rose-colored glasses, and it will be a good and healthy thing to do.

What if there was a gift in everything? What if in our everyday life, we could see the mounds of gifts that surround us moment by moment?

There's a fun story that I remember regarding this. I worked for a Mexican company hotel. The company was flying me to New York to get my American-Canadian perspective on the business. It serves mostly Mexicans, but the hotel also serves Americans and Canadians, and the company needed help on communicating and understanding the American and Canadian cultures, and how things worked. I was being flown to New York for a one-day mastermind meeting.

I was really excited to go. For some reason, I thought I had more time to check in because I only had a carry-on, but when I showed up at the airport they said, "Oh, sorry, we gave your ticket away. You will need to get another flight."

I ended up having to buy another flight to Mexico City. But then my new flight was delayed, and I knew that reaching my connection on time was going to be a miracle. But there was a chance.

At the terminal in Mexico City, I was trying to get to the right train to change terminals, and got five different answers. They all pointed me in the wrong direction. As I'm running through the halls I kept saying to myself, "Life is happening *for* me, life is happening *for* me." This continued on and on, until finally I got to the train and to my gate. Sure enough, the plane I needed was gone.

So I worked on the Diamond (the four-step process of changing your state). I breathed, and I smiled, and I breathed some more. And I said to myself, 'Okay, life is happening *for* me. There must be a gift in this.' I asked around, and I got a red-eye flight to New York. I wondered how I might function (I don't sleep on planes), but at least I would be there.

I chose to enjoy the flight. We landed in New York the minute the workshop was slated to begin. The stress was building up. But then I remembered again that there's a gift in everything. I looked around, looking for where my gift might be, as we waited at immigration.

A young woman in front of me seemed as if she might be the gift. I started talking with her and ended up sharing my crazy story. I was choosing to be in a good state. She completely surprised me when she said, "I can help you."

She steered me through the airport and navigated all the train ticket booths. She took me all the way to the taxi, which was glorious because she navigated all the train ticket booths. It was really nice to have the help and saved me a lot of time from having to figure it out myself. She brought me to the taxi and said, "This is as far as I can get you, but the taxi will take you to the door of the hotel." I gave her a huge hug and said, "You're amazing. Thank you so much."

In the back of the taxi, I changed into my dress and heels. I had been wearing leggings and flip flops. I changed carefully so that the driver couldn't see me, I could exit the taxi ready for the meeting, and not walk into the hotel looking like I had just come off a red-eye flight.

It was hilarious and I was laughing to myself thinking "I am changing in the back of the taxi. This is crazy." I was cracking myself up laughing. It was so much fun and I had the best time.

I entered the workshop and had a beautiful day and got to add a lot of value. What could have been a miserable situation ended up being a wonderful one—all from believing that there's a gift in everything. So I encourage you to look for the gift. Look for the gifts. Look for the piles of gifts that surround you at any given moment and enjoy them.

Steps and Methods

Here is how you can learn from my experience:

1. Become aware shit is hitting the fan.

To start, separate yourself from the shit that's happening. Become aware.

Now I know this seems obvious, but the obvious isn't always that obvious, and we tend to let our preset programs run the show. So wake up to the situation.

Work the Diamond. The first step is to change the position of your body by smiling, breathing, and moving it.

The second point is to change what you are focused on and ask yourself, "What am I thankful for?"

The third step is to replace the bullshit you are telling yourself, as in this instance, from 'I'm going to miss my flight' to 'Life is happening *for* me' and 'There is a gift in everything.'

And the fourth point of the Diamond is to connect to Source, know you are not alone, and ask for divine help.

Remind yourself that there is a gift in everything. This is the third step. I repeated this thought to myself often during this adventure. Let's do things differently. Let's remind ourselves that there is a gift in everything!

2. Literally look around you for the gift.

Ask yourself, "Where is the gift?" When I asked myself that, I got the answer of that wonderful girl. And in the taxi, I got the answer that I had a space to change into my dress to save time in preparation for my meeting. Where is the gift for *you*?

The outcome of this step is that when you take the time to look for the gifts, you'll find that they are everywhere.

3. Go with the flow of knowing and enjoying the constant gifts and be grateful.

Smile, knowing there is something magical to find. Knowing this makes life so much different. Use this process in everyday life. Look for the magic!

Find the magic. Keep looking, searching, discovering, and uncovering the magic that surrounds us every day. Perhaps the smile you see on someone's face, the smell of a baby's head, the dew on the grass, the gratitude of a friend, the breeze on our skin, the fact that our heart beats 100,000 times a day without us having to tell it to. That's magic. Look until you find it!

When you follow and implement these steps you will begin to see and understand that there is a gift in everything. Even though shit does occasionally hit the fan, there is a gift in every situation! Life can be a whole lot more fun when you're looking for gifts everywhere, as in my story of missing my flight to New York and how I was able to make lemonade out of lemons.

You will be able to do this, too, as you follow the three steps you're learning here:

- Become aware that shit is hitting the fan.
- Literally look around you for the gift in it.
- Go with the flow of knowing and enjoying the constant gifts, and be grateful.

When you wake up to the situation, you can separate yourself from it to be able to control your thoughts. Only then can you take the time to look for the gifts, and they are everywhere. Enjoy the magic that exists all around you! There is a gift in everything!

In our next chapter, we will explore the power of frequency.

 If you'd like further support from me, please use this QR. Looking forward to hearing from you!

Chapter 9

EVERYTHING HAS A FREQUENCY

Change your frequency, change your life.

Here I'll explore what frequency is. I'll look at the correlation of what frequencies match what emotions, and how changing our frequency changes our lives. I will share with you how frequency plays a part in our world and everything in it.

To illustrate this I will relate a story about my workplace, and working with sometimes-grumpy people. I'll also show you how to have an impact on the world in these three steps:

1. What frequency is.
2. What emotions resonate at what frequency.
3. How to raise your frequency and therefore change the world.

You'll discover from another perspective the two states of being crappy or happy. You'll get clear on what frequencies we are operating at, and learn the steps to changing your frequency. You will also learn the levels of frequency and how they affect your life. The higher the frequency the better your life will be.

Everything is energy. Everything is a vibration. Everything has a frequency. It's really interesting how frequency can be measured.

I am not a scientist, but it's proven by science now, that everything has a frequency, and that frequency affects everything. When you raise your frequency, you change your life. Low frequencies are fear, guilt, shame, etc., while the highest frequencies are unconditional love, joy and gratitude. They can all be measured and there are statistics to prove it. I'm going to share them with you here.

Do you ever feel helpless with what is going on in the world and what you can actually do? I keep coming back to the importance of raising our frequency. Raise your frequency, don't stay scared, don't be fearful. Don't be angry. This is low frequency. Low frequency begets low frequency, and we have a planet of people full of fear. What we can do is change our frequency to unconditional love. That means loving even the people you really don't want to. Love them. Be thankful, have gratitude. Love, joy, peace, and gratitude are the highest frequencies. The more we walk around with love and gratitude, the higher the frequency is.

There have been studies of meditation groups that have completely changed the course of violence in an area, because everyone is connected. My vibration affects you and your vibration affects me. This is why it's essential to choose who we spend time with, who we're spending our vibrations (or time) with, because we affect them and they affect us. It's a form of what's known as Bernoulli's principle, or the Law of Entrainment. The Law of Entrainment states that when two different frequencies are in the presence of one another, they will always come into resonance with each other; the lower frequency will move up to meet the higher one.

Being aware is similar to waking up and taking inventory on what you're thinking, and what your frequency is at that moment. Ask yourself, "What level am I? Am I at 10? Am I at a five on my attitude?" If you're at two vibrationally, you're attracting a whole lot of 2-energy and 2-material things, and 2-level drama. If you're at a 10 then you're attracting 10-energies and material things and blessings. It's just how it works.

We can raise our frequency. I experienced this firsthand on a daily basis when I worked in the vacation-ownership world. It is the easiest, hardest job. It's easy, because the hours are pretty good and you can make great money. But it's hard because everyone who comes in is determined not to buy from you. Not to listen, not to engage. Some people even make up big grand stories about their life that aren't even true. My job was just to break down the walls of resistance far enough so that people could peek over the wall and look at what I was offering them, so that they could make an educated choice. This wasn't easy, because a lot of people literally promised each other they weren't going to buy.

But who's responsible? I am. I'm responsible, I'm responsible for my frequency. I also know that my frequency can affect their frequency and I have the power to influence them. It was up to them whether they wanted to be influenced. But I had the ability to do that.

I knew I had to get my shit together first. I would literally go into the bathroom stall, smile, breathe and move and jump around to get my heart going.

I would also think about the things I'm thankful for and keep breathing, until I felt that my energy, my frequency, my vibration was at a 10, because that's what was necessary to get the job done. There was no way that I could get them over the line of change on the frequency chart if I was barely over the line myself. I needed to be way above the line in order to move them across the line. It was amazing how it worked. I would even get them standing up and breathing and jumping around at the presentation table.

I'm sure most of them thought I was nuts. I didn't care. I was responsible. I know what it takes to change your state. And so let's change it, let's at least get into the best possible position to make the best possible choice. With your kids and with your spouses, get them moving. Ask them what they're thankful for. Help them change their state. Have a dance party. There are so many different ways that you can raise your vibration, and frequencies. Change your frequency, change your life.

Frequency Scale

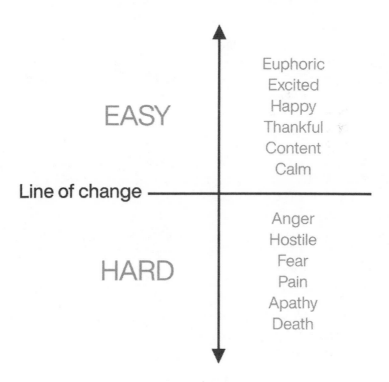

EASY

Euphoric
Excited
Happy
Thankful
Content
Calm

Line of change

Anger
Hostile
Fear
Pain
Apathy
Death

HARD

Here is how you can learn from me.

1. Learn what frequency is. It's important to get clear on this. Frequency is the rate at which a vibration occurs that constitutes a wave, either in a material (as in sound waves) or electromagnetic field (as in radio waves and light), usually measured per second. Humans are spiritual beings and each of us vibrates with a certain vibration. When we feel down, depressed, angry we have low vibration. The better and happier we feel, the higher our vibration, according to the philosopher David Hawkins.

Wayne Dyer says, "In essence, every single person, as well as large groups of people, can be calibrated for their energy levels." Generally speaking, low-energy people cannot distinguish truth from falsehood. They can be told how to think, whom to hate, whom to kill. They can be herded into a group-think mentality based on such trivial details as on what side of the river they were born, what their parents and their grandparents believed, the shape of their eyes, and hundreds of other factors having to do with appearance and total identification with their material world. Hawkins tells us that approximately 87 percent of humanity calibrates at a collective energy level that weakens them.

Ask yourself right now, "What is my frequency on a scale of 1-10?" Another way to ask is, "How am I feeling emotionally on a scale of 1-10?" This will give you the correct measurement as well. We are always vibrating at a certain frequency depending on how we think and therefore feel. The more we can become aware of our frequency the more we can consciously change it. Change your frequency, change your life.

Low vibration begets low vibration and high vibration begets high vibration. We've all experienced this in our life. If someone enters a room in a low vibrational state, most people can see it and feel it. And depending on the people in the room and level of awareness, that one person can bring down the energy of the whole room. The same is true when someone enters a room at a super high frequency. That one person can take a dud party and turn it into an awesome one in seconds, such as the example I shared with hiding in a bathroom stall for a few minutes to get my shit together and raise my frequency so that I could help my people raise their frequency high enough to be able to make a good choice for themselves. Write this down somewhere. Never make an important decision on a low frequency. Never ever ever. Always make important decisions in a high vibration.

In the frequency chart below you can see that there are levels of vibration. In the middle of the chart is the line of change. Anything below the line are low-frequency emotions like anger, fear, guilt.

The emotions above the line of change are the higher frequency emotions like peace, love, willingness.

There are only two states of being, crappy or happy. If you are below the line of change, you are in a crappy state. This is when you are thinking and feeling that life is hard. If you are above the line of change, you are in a happy state. This is when you feel that life is fun and easy. If you are around someone who is angry, how many steps — based on my simple chart — do they have to pass through to cross the line of change? They are just one step away. You need to be at least a couple steps above or more to be able to influence them energetically. This is why it's so important that we keep our frequency as high as possible. It affects ourselves and people around us.

In his book *Power vs Force*, Dr. David Hawkins explains the level of the impact the higher-vibration people make on other people. Here is his discovery:

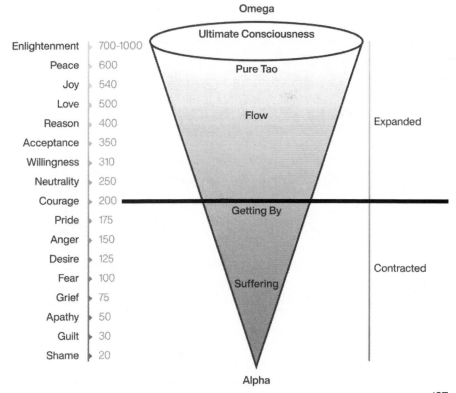

One individual who lives and vibrates to the energy of optimism and a willingness to be nonjudgmental of others will counterbalance the negativity of 90,000 individuals who calibrate at the lower weakening levels.

One individual who lives and vibrates to the energy of pure love and reverence for all of life will counterbalance the negativity of 750,000 individuals who calibrate at the lower weakening levels.

One individual who lives and vibrates to the energy of illumination, bliss, and infinite peace will counterbalance the negativity of 10 million people who calibrate at the lower weakening levels.

One individual who lives and vibrates to the energy of grace, pure spirit beyond the body, in a world of complete oneness, will counterbalance the negativity of 70 million people who calibrate at the lower weakening levels. The implications of these figures are immense for discovering ways of improving human consciousness. By raising your own frequency of vibration only slightly to a place where you regularly practice kindness, love, and receptivity, and where you see beauty and the endless potential of good in others as well as yourself, you counterbalance 90,000 people somewhere on this planet who are living in the low-energy levels of shame, anger, hatred, guilt, despair, and depression.

This is massively important! Change your frequency, change your life, change the world!

2. What emotions resonate at what frequency? The frequencies of low emotions are: shame, guilt, apathy, grief, fear, anger and pride to name a few.

The frequencies of the higher emotions are: willingness, acceptance, contentment, reason, love, joy, peace, enlightenment.

Which frequencies would you rather experience on a consistent basis? We have a choice. We are not victims to our emotions — we choose them. We all know people who have been through terribly hard situations and traumas who are miserable and we also know others who have been through similar situations and who are bright, shiny, happy lights of inspiration. What's the difference? Choice is the difference. Frequency is the difference. We have a choice.

What frequency are you at right now? Ask yourself based on the chart above, where are you honestly at right now with your frequency? If you are below the line of neutrality that means you are feeling like you are just getting by and are suffering. Where do you want to be? What would you rather be feeling? Look at the chart and choose what you would like to feel.

3. How to raise your frequency and therefore change the world. What is your emotional home? On a regular basis, discover where you are vibrationally. Breathe. Then ask yourself, "What is my favorite low-frequency go-to?" Anger, fear, sadness? Write down what comes to mind. Remember that the more you can deal with what is true, the more you are able to make the necessary changes. When I first discovered this, I realized that my emotional home was being stressed-out. This is every achiever's word for fear. When you are stressed-out, you are afraid of all that might not get done, in the most perfect way, at the best possible time etc. It's all fear.

Now ask yourself, "What is my high-frequency favorite?" When I'm above the line, where do I live? Write down what comes to mind. Be honest with yourself. Write down what is true.

Celebrate that you realized this. You are now aware of what is true! This is huge! So many people go their whole life not realizing that they are angry most of the time. If they fully knew they would likely seek how to change that. Remember that we are 95% subconscious, which means we are 95% program and your program may be mostly stress or anger or pain, etc. Knowing is the first beautiful step, so celebrate. Give yourself a hug or a high five or something for waking up and becoming aware!

Work the Diamond of Freedom. Again, the Diamond is a four-step process of getting your shit together and changing your state. The first step is to change the position of your body by smiling, breathing and moving it. The second point is to change what you are focused on and ask yourself "what am I thankful for?" The third step is to replace the bullshit you are telling yourself with what is true (if you feel shitty you have shitty thoughts). And the fourth point of the Diamond is to connect to the Source and ask for support!

This is what I would do in the bathroom stall preparing myself to help my clients. I'd smile, breathe, move around by running in place, tell myself I've got this, that I would find a way to help raise their frequency and I'd ask Source for help. It works! It's completely transformed my life for the better. I spend very little time suffering now, because I know how not to.

When you follow and implement these steps you will learn how to change your frequency, and therefore change your life. You will know the importance of getting clear on what frequency is. You will understand how frequency plays a part in our world and everything in it.

Low Frequency Has a Cost

Low frequency has a cost. Are you willing to pay the price? You hold the remote to your life.

Here I will share my story of living in fear, guilt, shame and anger, and then provide you steps for gaining clarity on where you are:

1. The pain and suffering from low frequency, and the long-term effects of low frequencies.
2. How low frequency has affected your life specifically.
3. How changing your frequency changes your life.

The outcome of this step is to show the science of what long periods of living in fear can cause a person, and to see and feel how fear and guilt and anger have affected your life and what it has cost you. You will know the difference between a happy or crappy life. You will learn the true cost to low vibrational energy and be inspired to raise it as high as you can.

Here's the thing about low frequency: fear, anger, guilt and shame are terrible things to experience. This was my frequency for years. I was terrified and I had so much guilt and shame, about leaving the Mission organization I was with, about my unsuccessful, abusive marriage.

Leaving the Mission was huge. I chose to do things differently, and to live a freer life away from the rules and dictation of the Mission. It was wonderful, but it was also terrible because I still felt guilty. That's how you control people, make them feel guilty. Shame is even worse. Shame means you ARE bad. Not that you did something bad, but that you, at your core, are bad.

It was years before I let myself off the hook and realized that it was bullshit, that this was not how God operated. Unconditional love is who God is. And guilt, shame, fear, control — that is not God.

I started redefining and getting to know God in a different way. I realized the physical impact those low frequencies had on me as well. Over a year and a half I had one constant migraine, where I'd be curled up in a ball in a dark room for hours.

I'd always been prone to headaches, mostly because of my diet. But since I've changed that, my headaches are gone. But the migraines were on another level. When I was suffering from a migraine, I was barely a human being with the amount of pain that I was in. One day, for the first time in my life, I actually looked at a bottle of pills and went "Hmm...I could end the pain right now..." I sucked in air when it hit me. "I can't believe I just thought that." And so now I understand a little, about how people get to the point of killing themselves, like my grandmother did when she was in an abusive relationship and didn't feel like there was a way out. She took a pile of pills and ended her life. At that moment, holding those pills, I understood her. Low frequency has a cost.

There are many studies that show the physical component of a specific emotional charge. People suffering from chronic pain know how it's a vicious circle because with the pain, it's really hard to be in a high frequency. But raising your frequency is the answer.

The cost isn't just in the pain that you feel. It's the loss of who you are as a person. I wasn't able to take care of my kids in the best way that I could. I was barely surviving. That brought on more guilt and shame. There were also financial costs. I ended up driving to my wonderful uncle and aunt's house a couple of hours away and stayed with them for three days a week for a year, so that I could go to an acupuncture migraine clinic, four times a day. My second husband and my parents were amazing at helping me take care of the boys. It affected my family big time.

What changed was that I raised my vibration. I removed the fear. I moved to Mexico where I could start over and not be trapped by the Mission with its rules, judgment, guilt and shame — and most of all, escaping the fear of my abusive ex-husband. I was able to raise my frequency. I was able to live in unconditional love and gratitude. You can do that too, even amid your pain.

Be aware of what's going on that's causing you to have this pain. Figure out how you can change that and raise the frequency so that you can get relief and so that you can truly live.

Here is how you can learn from my experiences.

Step 1. Study the pain, suffering, long-term effects of low frequency.

Many studies show that the field of frequency (known as "the field") all around us affects matter directly. One study was on a group of women who all had ovarian cancer markers (signs of inclination towards cancer) in the field. Some had ovarian cancer initially, but eventually all who had the marker in the field eventually had ovarian cancer. In other words, cancer didn't create the marker in the field. The marker in the field created the cancer.

This is super important to understand. What this means is that our frequency affects our physical bodies, not just how we feel about our day. At the 2017 Neuroscience Education Institute (NEI) Congress, a session focused on the physiology of fear and its impact on wellness. It was presented by Mary D. Moller, PhD, DNP, ARNP, PMHCNS-BC, CPRP, FAAN, associate professor, Pacific Lutheran University School of Nursing, and director of Psychiatric Services, Northwest Center for Integrated Health. The potential effects of chronic fear on physical health include headaches turning into migraines, muscle aches turning into fibromyalgia, body aches turning into chronic pain, and difficulty breathing turning into asthma, said Moller.

The potential effects of chronic fear on emotional health include: Dissociation from self, an inability to have loving feelings, learned helplessness, phobic anxiety, mood swings, obsessive-compulsive thoughts.

This is just a part of the damage that long-term fear can do to the body. I needed to wake up! I had been living in fear for over 10 years before I started getting help for it. It's time to pay attention to our energy, our frequency, our vibration. I began listening to different healing frequencies on YouTube to cleanse me, and help me raise my frequency. For example, the 741 Hz frequency is known for its ability to penetrate deeply into the conscious and subconscious mind. This frequency is very beneficial for helping remove toxins and electromagnetic radiation from your cells. In doing so, this frequency can cleanse your cells from viral, bacterial and fungal infections. This makes regular listening of 741 Hz a crucial tool in your arsenal.

Ask yourself, "How much time do I spend in fear? How is fear affecting my life?" Write down anything that comes to mind, without judgment.

The effects of long-term anger on the body are: headache, digestion problems, insomnia, increased anxiety, depression, high blood pressure, skin problems such as eczema, heart attack and stroke.

I held quite a bit of anger in me as I was not taught how to deal with anger or even express it. But people do get angry. If we don't deal with anger, we store it in our bodies and it turns into disease. I have spent a lot of time with my coach/healer, working through my anger. In my mind, now that I know the harmful effects, there is no other option but to deal with it. Ask yourself, "How much time do I spend angry?" Write down anything that comes to mind, without judgment.

The effects of shame on the body include: anxiety, depression, worthless-ness, low self-esteem.

People who are consistently ashamed live out a difficult, emotional and mental battle every day. Ask yourself, "How much time do I spend in shame?" Write down anything that comes to mind, without judgment.

Step 2. How have frequencies affected your life, specifically?

Ask yourself, "How has low-frequency emotions like fear affected my life?" Write down anything that comes to mind. For me it caused major debilitating migraines where I had to live in a dark room curled up in a ball in excruciating pain on tons of pain meds for a year and a half.

Ask yourself, "How have low-frequency emotions affected me, my family, my work, my finances?" Write down anything that comes to mind, without judgment. In my case it cost me my job, a year & half of my life, cost me not being able to be the mom I wanted and needed to be for my kids, cost me thousands and thousands of dollars, and most of all, it cost me loving my life.

Ask yourself, "Is it worth it for me to continue in low-frequency emotions?" Write down the answer. If the answer is no, it's not worth it, then make a deci-sion right now to do things differently. Make it your mission to figure out how to stay as much as possible in a high frequency of joy, love and gratitude.

The outcome of this step is to really see and feel how fear and guilt and anger have affected your life and all that it has cost you.

Step 3. Change your frequency, change your life.

Meditation is a wonderful way to raise your frequency and there are many studies that show the benefits not only individually but also collectively in helping specifically to reduce crime. Here is an example. A study published in the *Journal of Health and Environmental Research* suggests that practicing the Transcendental Meditation® technique and its advanced program, the TM-Sidhi® program may lead to reduced societal stress, as reflected in reduced rates of murder and violence. This group practice is said to create a positive effect in the environment due to a hypothesized "field effect of consciousness."

Between 2007 and 2010, the size of the TM-Sidhi group located at Maharishi University of Management in Fairfield, Iowa, was above or near 1,725 participants, the size predicted to have a positive influence on the U.S. quality of life. This predicted threshold represents the square root of 1% of the US population at that time. Dr. Michael Dillbeck, a co-author of the study, adds "This study and 17 other peer-reviewed studies suggest that one's individual consciousness is directly connected to an underlying, universal field of consciousness, and that by collectively enlivening that universal field through the Transcendental Meditation technique, such a group can have a positive effect on the quality of life in society."

The study found that a slightly increasing trend in murder rate during the baseline period 2002 to 2006 shifted significantly to a declining trend during the four-year period 2007 through 2010. AAs a result of a monitored, significant increase of Transcendental Meditation sessions, the urban murder rate was reduced 28.4% relative to the 2002-2006 average. The researchers estimated 4,136 murders in the 206 cities were averted by the significantly increased use of Transcendental Meditation sessions.

The authors of the study calculated that there was a 1 in 10 million trillion probability that the reduced trend in murder rates could simply be due to chance.

If you want to find the secrets of the universe, think in terms of energy, frequency, and vibration." — Nikola Tesla.

And so, what are the seven healing frequencies?

Healing Frequencies

There are many different healing frequencies. Here are a few to try on for yourself.

The Solfeggio Frequencies

174 Hz   — relieves pain and stress.
285 Hz   — heals tissues and organs.
396 Hz   — liberates you from fear and guilt.
417 Hz   — facilitates change.
528 Hz   — for transformation and DNA repair.
639 Hz   — reconnects you with your relationships.
741 Hz   — helps provide solutions and self-expression.

When you follow and implement these steps, you will learn that low frequency has a cost. You will know the importance of taking a good look at how low frequency impacts the world and see where these low frequencies have affected you personally. The best way to change the world is to raise our frequency, including the following steps:

- Understand the long-term effects of pain and suffering as a result of low frequencies.
- Determine how low frequencies have affected your life specifically.

Change your frequency, change your life.

The outcome of this step is to show the science of what long periods of living in fear can cause in a person, and to see and feel how fear and guilt and anger have affected your life and what it has cost you. You will know the facts about frequency and how it is the difference between a happy or crappy life. You will learn the true cost to low vibrational energy and by staring the aftermath straight in the face, hopefully you will be inspired to raise it as high as you can.

Next, we will look at your basic human needs.

 If you'd like further support from me, please use this QR.
Looking forward to hearing from you!

Chapter 10

THE BASIC HUMAN NEEDS

Having needs is not evidence of weakness, but of humanity.

We are more the same than you think. What if we actually understood ourselves and others?

Here I will explore the seven basic human needs. I will discuss how you should know your top two or three operational needs, which you may not have been aware that you can change.

To illustrate this, I will share a story of how I use each of these basic human needs.

Then you will receive a series of steps that will help you comprehend and use the human needs. I will also provide you with steps that you can use:

1. Learn the seven human needs.
2. Realize the two or three that you need the most and how these affect your life choices.
3. The two to three needs you want now to take your life to the next level.

You will see that we humans are really very similar in our needs and that we all have needs that are more important than others, that dictate how we make choices. You will learn how to take control of your life. You tell yourself how to be and what to do. You will then be able to choose the ones you want to consciously operate under moving forward!

What if we actually understood ourselves and others? What if we're really not that different as humans? What if we're really a lot the same across cultures and languages? I believe we are. I have been to 56 countries, and one of the main reasons I wanted to travel with my kids was to show them the world, and to experience that humans are humans.

We all have needs and wants and desires. There are seven in total. Here I have adapted what I learned from Tony Robbins.

The first human need that I'm going to talk about is the need for certainty. The need to know what's going on, the need to have a plan. When I get stressed, I need certainty more than normally. I need to control because I feel like I'm losing control. That's how certainty plays out in a nonbeneficial way for me. In a beneficial way for me, I'm pretty, organized.

The next need is the need for variety, the need to mix things up. This is one of my favorite needs. I love changing things up, I go to different restaurants, I park in different parking spots. I love going to different countries. When I go on vacation, I'm known to hit eight countries in one vacation. In a nonbeneficial way, it has affected me by moving through relationships too quickly. Because I need variety, I get bored.

The next need is the need for significance, the need to be noticed, to feel important. There's nothing wrong with this. There's a beneficial way and a nonbeneficial way to meet each need. I was in denial about this need in me. But I came to see that it also means being valued and appreciated. This is why I had to achieve, achieve, achieve. I had to be the best. This has been a major theme in my life. Achieve, achieve, achieve. Next milestone, next trophy, next accomplishment. Next pat on the back.

The fourth need is for love and connection. This is my highest need. I didn't love myself for years. So I looked outside myself to find it. That affected my relationships, because I was choosing for my needs to be met. I was choosing unconsciously. Again, there's a way for that to be beneficial and a way for it not to be beneficial and, and the need for love and connection is expressing love and being loved. It's a beautiful thing. We all need it.

The fifth need is the need to express yourself and speak the truth. There's so much deception, and we crave being able to be truthful, and to receive the truth. I really felt this in leaving the Mission organization I was part of for the first 30 years of my life. I experienced this in the process of giving myself permission to write this book. Some people may be hurt or offended by this, but I choose to be free. We need to speak the truth to ourselves, because so often we lie to ourselves. We have a need for the truth.

The sixth human need is the need to be aware, to wake up, to listen to your intuition, to become aware of new information, to grow. I've been able to work on my intuition in the last eight years through my coach. And to trust it. I didn't trust myself for years, because I chose to marry Joe, who turned out to be abusive. I ended up in an abusive marriage for 7.5 years. Holy shit, how can I be trusted to choose anything again? And so I had to really work on trusting my intuition, the Holy Spirit in me, the Source in me.

The seventh need is your connection to all, to know and understand that we are all connected. We are not completely separate individuals. Energy connects us. When we forget this we create separation and we feel terrible.

I had a beautiful relationship with a man. Once when he was working down at the beach, I was at home and having a hard time. He texted me and asked, "Are you okay?" I was not okay. But I knew he was working, and that if I said I wasn't okay, this would affect his work. I didn't want to do that. And so I was not authentic. I said, "No, I'm fine." I used a cool trick. I broke the energetic cords between us by saying, "They are to them, I am to me, back with love." They are to them (you can use their name), I am to me, back with love. I did that three times.

When he came home a few hours later, he asked, "Are you okay? There was this moment where I didn't feel you anymore. You were gone, I thought we were done."

I was shocked! I told him how I did the cord-cutting thing. He said, "Please don't ever do that again."

I could go on and on with how we are all connected. I know many of you have had the experience of thinking about your mom, and then next thing you know your mom calls or you go to text someone and then all of a sudden they're texting you in that moment. It's because we're connected. We have a need to connect, we have a need to remember that we are connected, instead of believing the program that we are all disconnected and separate.

My top three needs were love, significance and variety. When you know the seven needs, you can consciously choose which ones you want to have, as your top two or three needs.

We have a choice. We don't have to be run by the program. So my new top three needs are love, awareness/growth, and connection to all. As a result, my life choices are about learning and growing and becoming more aware and listening to my intuition, so that I can contribute to the people around me. I changed careers, I no longer make myself crazy with needing to achieve. I am now saying no to things. I'm following my intuition. I live my life completely differently because I'm consciously choosing which needs to meet and to meet them in a beneficial way. I'm so thankful! I love my life.

Here is how you can learn from my experiences.

Step 1. Learn the 7 Human Needs.

To start, determine your certainty. The first human need is the need for certainty. Ask yourself, "Where in my life do I need certainty?" Write down anything that comes to mind without judgment. Keep repeating the question until you have at least three to five examples.

Understand variety. The second human need is the need for variety, or the need for uncertainty. Ask yourself, "Where in my life do I need variety?" Write down anything that comes to mind, without judgment.

Figure out significance. The third human need is the need for significance, the need for recognition, the need to be noticed and praised. Ask yourself, "Where in my life do I need significance?" Write down at least three to five examples, without judgment.

The need for love. The fourth human need is the need for love and/or connection. Some people don't know what love is and so they settle for connection. This human need shows up in the form of needed human relationships, touch, words, etc. Ask yourself, "Where in my life do I need love and connection?" Write down anything that comes to mind, without judgment.

The fifth human need is the need for the truth and self-expression. This shows up in the form of the need to hear and express the truth. Ask yourself, "Where in my life do I need truth and to express myself?" Write down anything that comes to mind without judgment, and come up with three to five examples.

The need for awareness. The sixth human need is the need for awareness. The need to learn and grow. The need to be aware so you can follow your intuition. This shows up in the form of listening to your intuition, your inner voice, your higher self, the holy spirit. Ask yourself, "Where in my life do I need awareness?" Write down anything that comes to mind without judgment. Come up with three to five examples.

The need for connection. The seventh human need is the need to remember that we are all connected. That we have a connection to all things. That we are in fact not separate from each other. This shows up in the form of feeling connected to others and to the source, when you take care of each other, when you contribute to someone, when you help animals. When you truly understand that we are all connected it makes you want to contribute to the whole. We sometimes forget we're connected to each other. Ask yourself, "Where in my life do I see and feel connection to all things?" Come up with at least three to five examples.

Step 2. Realize what two to three needs you need the most and how meeting those needs affected your life choices.

Here's how you can do it.

Ask yourself, "What are my top two or three human needs?" When I first did this exercise, mine were love, significance, and variety. Write down anything that comes to mind without judgment.

What is their order of importance? Ask yourself, "What is the order of importance of these needs for me?" This means, in a way, how you're living your life operationally and what shows up the most in terms of needs.

Ask yourself, "How have those needs in that order affected my life?" Seek the truth and you will find it. For me the truth was that love being first was great in many ways, as I have had a wonderful life loving on others and being loved in return, but it also caused me to seek love outside of myself and sometimes in an unhealthy way, instead of understanding I have all the love I need inside of my self. The need for significance highly affected my life because I was often in work and achievement mode in order to be recognized and get my need for significance met. I realized too that the recognition also made me feel worthy of love and therefore fed my need for love. It also served me in many ways as I have accomplished much in my life. The need for variety helped me have the adventurous life that I've had. It helped me in my escape to Mexico, in moving to multiple different countries and cultures over the years.

Step 3. What 2-3 needs do you choose to take your life to the next level?

Ask yourself, "What two or three needs will take my life to the next level?" Make sure you keep breathing through this process. Go over the definitions of the seven needs. Write down whatever comes to mind.

Ask yourself, "What order of importance should they be in?" The correct order for me is love, awareness, and connection. What is the order for your needs?

Ask yourself, "What would change in my life if I made these my top three needs?" Write down anything that comes to mind. For me, making that change has absolutely changed my life. It's one of the reasons I'm now writing this book. It wasn't as important to me before because my focus was on love from outside, significance, and adventure and variety. Now it's love from inside, learning to be more aware, learning and growing so that I can contribute to all.

When you follow and implement these steps you will realize that we are more the same than you think. You will see that it's possible to understand ourselves and others. You will also understand that you can consciously change the needs. You will then be able to choose the ones you want to consciously operate under moving forward!

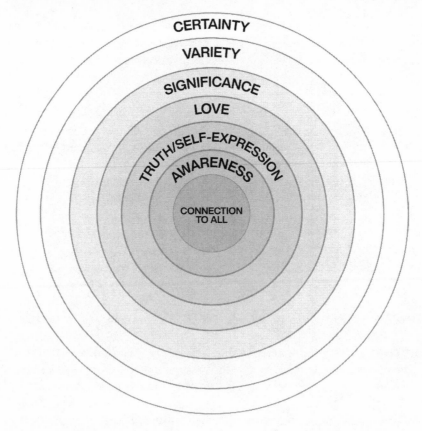

Is It the Lot of Man to Suffer?

Why are we addicted to suffering?

Here I'm exploring beneficial and non beneficial ways to meet our needs. We get addicted to a behavior if it meets three of our needs at a high level (nonbeneficial). We can also get addicted to a behavior if it meets three of our needs at a high level (beneficial). With awareness we can meet our own needs in a beneficial way.

I will illustrate this with a story about the rampant violence around the world.

You will then get some steps to navigate your needs and addictions:

1. Two ways to meet your needs, both beneficial and nonbeneficial.
2. Reasons why we are addicted and when to realize we are.
3. Meet the need in a beneficial way.

In doing all of this, you will have a complete chart of examples of how you meet your beneficial and nonbeneficial needs. You will realize that when you are addicted to a behavior it's because you're trying to meet your needs. But we have a choice. We can meet our own needs beneficially. Period. You will learn and see how you have been addicted to your own suffering and how it's affected you and the people around you.

Have you ever met someone addicted to their suffering? Could that person in some way be you? It certainly was me for a period of time. And now that I understand the seven human needs, I can understand better, why we do what we do, and how we will do anything to meet our needs, even if it's self sabotage.

I was super addicted to my story of being a single mom, raising two kids alone, and being abandoned by the Mission and having to run and hide for my life. Many things fed into this idea of "poor me." I saw that I was meeting my needs for love and significance this way. I got a lot of love sharing my story. And I got a lot of significance, because it was not just a small thing that happened, it was a big thing. The way I viewed it and my perspective on it made it worse than it needed to be. I now know how it feels to be on the other side of that belief system. I can look back on those things now and shrug my shoulders and go, "Yeah, okay. It happened, I learned a lot and it was a blessing in lots of ways." We have to see what we're doing and how we're behaving to meet our needs.

Remember, there's a beneficial way and a nonbeneficial way. It's hard to see the nonbeneficial way of love. But it was easy for me to see since I stayed with people longer than I should have because I wanted love. I should have left my abusive ex-husband Joe years earlier. But I was holding on thinking that maybe one day he would love me because marriage was supposed to be loving. Then I saw that it was he who was choosing to live in that abusive way. I understand now that he didn't understand love.

So we will meet our needs, however we need to meet them. Even if it means hurting somebody else, hurting ourselves. Think about the violence that we have in the world today. Why is it so prominent? What needs does violence meet in the world? What need was the man who stabbed my friend Dani filling? He was meeting a need for certainty that he'd get money. And attention - significance. Didn't he have Dani's 100% attention at that moment? He was connected to her literally, with a knife in her belly. He had her 100% attention. And then you could also throw some variety in there. Because he didn't know at what time someone would walk in or what point her daughter would come down the stairs again.

There's some variety in there too. So that's four needs that are being met at a high level, and when three or four needs are being met at a high level, we become addicted. One day I was playing football with the kids in a big pool. I threw a football. An amazing spiral, perfect, right in the pocket across the pool, right into the arms of the kids. And I caught myself looking around to see if anyone noticed. And I started laughing out loud. Because I became aware that I was looking for my need for significance to be met.

I wanted someone to notice how amazing I just threw the football. And so instead of continuing to look around, I gave myself a pat on the back and said that was amazing. It was a really fun reminder of how we are meeting our needs all day long in different ways. If we can wake up and separate ourselves from it, then we can see it, then we can make a change. And here's the thing, now that you know, you will see it in others... you're gonna see it everywhere. Now you're gonna say "Oh, they're looking for significance. Oh, they're looking for love. Oh, wow. I think they need some variety." We pick fights with our significant others because we're bored. We need variety. And we don't care how we get it.

So rather than offering to go out for a walk, to go see a movie, we pick a fight.

What if we were aware enough to go "Wait a second. I don't want to fight about your socks on the floor. I'm bored. Can we mix it up instead? Can we go do something different?" What if we could do that?

It's an amazing way to live when you're aware. It's so fun. To not be running on the program but to be choosing. To be choosing what you think and how you feel and how you're going to respond instead of being controlled by the program/your elephant.

Here is how you can learn from me.

7 Human Needs

1   What are the ways you get Certainty? Uncertainty?

Certainty		Variety	
Beneficial	Non-Beneficial	Beneficial	Non-Beneficial

2   What are the ways you get Significance? Love/Connection?

Significance		Love/Connection	
Beneficial	Non-Beneficial	Beneficial	Non-Beneficial

Step 1. There are two ways to meet your needs.

To start, list the first four human needs as they are of the Personality. The last three needs are of the Spirit. We will not include them in this exercise. Write down on a separate piece of paper or fill in the chart provided the Four Needs of the Personality

Ask yourself, "How do I meet each need beneficially?" Write down anything that comes to mind without judgment. Seek the truth and you will find it. I met my needs beneficially by being organized — certainty. Traveling the world, able to adjust to new environments fairly easily — variety. Working hard and accomplishing amazing things — significance. Loving people fiercely and receiving love in return — love. Speaking my truth and living it out openly and authentically — truth. Following my intuition and protecting my boys — awareness. Contributing to the world by sharing my gifts and talents and helping others to live extraordinary lives — connection.

Ask yourself, "How do I meet each need nonbeneficially?" Write down anything that comes to mind without judgment. I met my needs nonbeneficially for example by being controlling — certainty. Getting bored easily — variety. I met my need for significance nonbeneficially by needing to be number one. I stayed with a few relationships way too long because I just wanted to be loved — love. I would express myself too much and with force, or would hold back what I needed to say to appease — truth. Sometimes my desire to grow would be at the expense of my family by being away a lot — awareness. Sometimes I just plain forget that we are all connected — connection to all.

Step 2. Realize the reasons why we are addicted to certain behaviors.

Here's how you can do it.

Ask yourself, "What behavior am I addicted to?" Write down anything that comes to mind. Common answers are smoking, feeling stressed out, worried, controlling, obsessive, angry, eating unhealthy foods, etc.

Ask yourself, "What three needs is this addictive behavior meeting at a high level?" Write down whatever comes to mind. I used the example of Dani's attacker.

Ask yourself, "How is this hurting me?" For Dani's attacker, the cost was that he ended up in jail, probably the rest of his life. For some addictive behaviors it could mean major sickness, death, unhappiness. Get real with yourself here.

The outcome of this step is to realize where you are also addicted to a behavior in order to meet your needs.

Step 3. Meet the need in a beneficial way.

Here's what you can do.

Wake up to the fact you are meeting a nonbeneficial need. I suggest you go back through the steps and ask the questions again to see what other nonbeneficial needs you are meeting. This is YOUR life! You get to design it if you want. Or you can let the program design it for you. Which is it?

Celebrate that you just became aware. Every time you become aware that you are meeting a need in a nonbeneficial way or in a beneficial way, celebrate!

Ask yourself, "How can I meet this need in a beneficial manner?" I realized that I had thrown the football in a beautiful spiral and was looking for significance in getting recognition. I instead laughed and patted myself on the back mentally and said great job Amy, that was awesome.

When you follow and implement these steps you will learn why you are addicted to suffering. Walk away with a complete chart of examples of how you meet your beneficial and nonbeneficial needs. You will learn and see how you have been addicted to your own suffering and how it's affected you and the people around you.

Awaken Enlightenment Within (Understanding Chakras)

What if there were more to the body than meets the eye?

Here I will explore the seven energy centers. We need to maintain these energy centers in order to live optimally.

To illustrate, I will share with you the story of how I realized my heart and solar plexus were blocked.

You will also learn the three steps to having a system flowing freely energetically:

1. Learn there are seven energy centers that match up with the seven human needs.
2. Each center needs to flow freely to run optimally and they each get blocked with specific emotions.
3. Crying, realization, changing your thoughts, energy work modalities can all help unblock a chakra.

In the end you will know and understand the seven chakras, how they line up with the seven human needs, and how they can get blocked and unblocked. You will have a better idea of how to help yourself and others when needed.

Have you ever thought that there might be more to the body than meets the eye? Have you ever watched a documentary that teaches you about the body and you're like, "Whoa, I didn't know that. That's crazy." How does our heart beat 100,000 times a day? Amazing things. What I am about to share with you is a little like that.

There are seven energy centers in the body that we are not taught about in our Western schools. Elsewhere in the world, such as Asia and India, people are taught this. Everyone has energy centers known as chakras. Here are the seven main chakras:

- Root
- Sacral
- Solar Plexus
- Heart
- Throat
- Third Eye
- Crown

I realized that my heart and my solar plexus were blocked. You may wonder what that means. Have you ever woken up and felt a little off? Once we understand we have energy centers, and we understand that we need to maintain those energy centers no different than any other organ or anything else to do with the body. Energy centers get blocked by different emotions.

This will become clear shortly. The root chakra, the need for certainty, is blocked by fear, which is one of the lowest frequencies. The more frightened you are, the more you're messing up your root chakra, which puts you into survival mode.

The second chakra, the sacral/sexual chakra, the need for variety, is blocked by guilt and shame. And when you think about all the guilt and shame that surrounds sex, you can understand why so many people's sexual chakras are compromised, are not flowing freely. People are not in their flow, they are not in their creativity, they're not rolling with the punches, they are stressed out, afraid, worried and feel guilty.

The third chakra is your solar plexus, which is the one I had issues with. Mostly because it was blocked by anger. The solar plexus is right below your rib cage, the top of your belly. I didn't even know I was so angry. In the culture where I grew up, I wasn't allowed to be angry. So I would stuff my anger down, and it would turn into sadness, because that's what was accepted better, but anger? I didn't express my anger and so it was all stuffed and held in my belly.

My heart was also blocked. The heart gets blocked from grief. I had my share of grief, losing my marriage, eight years of abuse, violence, anger. I think I might have been the reason a baby died once, during my missionary days in Papua New Guinea. She was newly born and she had pneumonia. And the family was already wailing, because they believed she was dead. We were doing all that we could do.

My partners asked me to go grab the medicine, and so I tore through the jungle, up to my partner's house to get the adrenaline, stomping through the jungle in my boots, in the wet grass and mud. I get back all out of breath and I'm reading the instructions on how much of the medicine to give. I missed a zero, and gave the wrong instructions, and the baby got too much, and she died. I felt immense grief and guilt for not being better, for getting worried and stressed so that I couldn't think straight, so that I made a mistake. I blocked my sacral and heart chakra both in that situation.

Then there was the grief of the Mission abandoning me, the grief of friends stealing from me and then disappearing. I had experienced quite a bit of grief and my heart was blocked. There was this one day I remember when I was struggling with my unofficially adopted son Zander. I took him in at 16 and raised him until he was 19. We went to our healer Josh to get some help. At the end of the session, he looked at Zander and he said, "Zander, follow your intuition and tell Amy whatever it is you feel you need to tell her."

He took a deep breath, and he said, "You have this incredible heart, this huge heart that everyone can see, and everyone can feel. And then there's this inner heart that you don't let anyone else touch or allow in."

My first reaction was to think, "No. I live my life out in front of everybody I love freely." And then I asked myself to listen to the truth. A few days later I realized he was right. I had a rock in the middle of my heart that I protected because I didn't want to get hurt. That's what grief can do.

There are different modalities that you can use to help clear your chakras. The main one that I use and do almost every day is yoga. Yoga not only helps your muscles but your chakras. Yoga aligns your chakras and cleans your chakras so that you can be as optimal as possible. Another way to clear your chakras is to cry. I have cried at this point, honestly, for hundreds of hours. I didn't cry for years, I kept it all in until someone would die in the village and I would wail with them. Living in Papua New Guinea as a missionary for four-and-a-half years with an abusive husband was tough and only when some-one died would I give myself permission to cry.

I would wail. I didn't understand wailing. Westerners don't grieve properly in my opinion. Tribal people grieve properly. I would do that with them. I wasn't just crying for the death in the village, I was crying also for me, and for my boys and what we were living with. But that wasn't very often. And so all the other times I would hold it in, because if I cried, things got worse for me. And most of all, I had to keep my kids safe. protected. So I didn't cry, I didn't yell. That's the other thing you can do to clear your chakras, you can yell, you can get angry, you can punch some pillows. The thing is to do it in a way that's safe, in a way that you're not hurting anybody. I go out into the desert and I scream my head off, it feels so good. Be angry. Sometimes you need to be angry, sometimes things make you angry and sad.

Get it out. Don't let it stay in because if you keep it in, it messes up your energy centers/chakras. And you've got to take care of your chakras no different than you take care of the rest of your body. The other thing you can do is get help. Go to a healer, go to an energy worker. Again, we are all energy. There are people who know how to do that. Sometimes things take work and consistent therapy. And sometimes things can be healed in a second. So seek to understand what could help you and think about whether or not you have had fear, guilt or shame, anger, grief, or lies in your life.

There are so many different ways that you can use to help maintain your energy centers. Meditation and Breathwork are other beautiful ways of clearing and helping your energy centers work in the best possible way for you.

Here is how you can learn from my experiences.

Step 1. Learn the 7 energy centers that match up with the 7 human needs.

I do this step by sharing the story of how I realized my heart and solar plexus were blocked.

To start, understand the chakras.

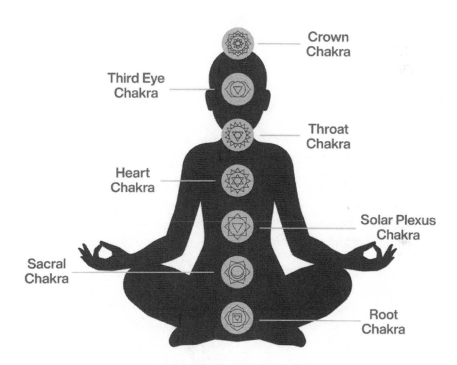

The first chakra is the **root chakra.** This lines up with certainty, the first human need. The root chakra is all about survival. It's all about taking care of our primal needs. Which matches up with certainty, needing to know, needing to plan. Your primal Root Chakra is down at the bottom, it's at the base, basically, right below and over your private parts. And the color for that is red. Sacral. The sacral chakra is just below your belly button and it's orange. That is the sexual chakra that meets the need of variety. You don't want sex to be mechanical, you want it to flow and the sacral chakra is all about flowing and being creative. We need that in our life. We need certainty and we need survival and we need to have flow, we need to be creative, all of it is necessary.

Solar Plexus. The third chakra is your solar plexus. It's yellow and matches the need for significance. Your solar plexus is where your will and your fire and your motivation comes from, from your core, from your center. It's located right below your ribs, top of your stomach.

Heart. Your heart chakra is the fourth center. It's green and matches love and connection. It is located in the center of your chest. This is also a center for creating. We all have the need for love and connection.

Throat. This is the fifth chakra, which is colored blue and is the counterpart to your need to express the truth not only to yourself but to others.

Third Eye. This is the sixth chakra, located in the center of your head. It's the eye that sees without your eyes open (the third eye), and that matches the need for awareness, the need to follow your intuition, the need to grow, the need to wake up and get off the program.

Crown. The seventh is the crown chakra, at the top of your head. It is the counterpart to connection to all, this is where you realize that we are all one. There is no separation.

Step 2. Each center needs to flow freely to run optimally and they each get blocked with specific emotions.

We need to maintain these energy centers in order to live optimally.

Here's how the energy centers are blocked:

Root — Blocked by fear. The more scared you are, the more that you are messing up your root chakra, which is putting you into survival mode. Ask yourself, "Where in my life have I been so afraid that I know it affected me?" Write down anything that comes to mind. For me I was the most afraid when I ran away with my kids from my abusive husband.

Sacral — Blocked by guilt and shame. The sacral chakra — the need for variety — is blocked by guilt and shame. Ask yourself, "When have I felt so much guilt and shame that I know it's affected me?" For me I felt the most guilt and shame when I decided to not live my life single and alone and went against the church/Mission organization I was in and started to date again.

Solar plexus — Blocked by anger. The third chakra is your solar plexus. Mostly it's blocked by anger. Ask yourself, "When have I felt so much anger that I know it's affected me?" Write down anything that comes to mind. I experienced the most anger being mad at Joe for his abuse and at God for a while. I was mad that he made me a girl, that he would "allow" me to get into an abusive marriage, have to run to be safe, and have to start over alone.

Heart — Blocked by grief. When sadness is not expressed it can severely affect your heart. It creates a protective shell and it keeps you closed off to fully giving and receiving love. Ask yourself, "When have I felt so much grief, that I know it's affected me?" Write down anything that comes to mind. I experienced the most grief over the death of my marriage, my community shunning me and over the death of the baby because of my mistake.

Throat —Blocked by lies. If you've been telling others or yourself lies your throat chakra probably needs some attention. The throat chakra will also get blocked if you are lying to others as well. Breathe deep into your lungs again and ask your higher self, "When have I lied to myself or others so much that I know it's affected me?" Write down anything that comes to mind. The biggest lie of my life was telling myself that I didn't have value.

Third Eye — Blocked by not following your intuition. Breathe deep into your lungs again and ask your higher self, "When have I not listened to my intuition, my Higher Self, so much that I know it's affected me?" Write down anything that comes to mind. It's hard to admit, but I didn't listen to Source in me about marrying my second husband. I knew, deep down it wasn't what I should be doing, but I did it anyway to give myself a loving husband and a dad for the boys.

Crown — Blocked by forgetting we are all connected. Breathe deep into your lungs again and ask your higher self, "When have I completely forgotten that I am connected to all, so much, that I know it's affected me?" Write down anything that comes to mind. I didn't realize that we were all connected, and I used to eat meat. I now choose not to kill animals in order to eat.

The hope is that you will realize that it's important to take care of your energy centers and make sure they are flowing freely.

Step 3. Crying, realization, changing your thoughts, energy work modalities can all help unblock a chakra.

Here's what you can do.

Yoga. Yoga has changed my life. I was super resistant to it at first, but now I love it and can totally appreciate what it does for my mind, body and energy sessions. If you don't already do yoga consistently, I encourage you to get started with a month of classes. Best to have a teacher to start so that you can make sure you are doing the positions correctly. Call a person you know who does yoga already and get their recommendation and then book it. Right now, do it.

Crying. Another great way to cleanse and clear the energy centers is to cry. Sometimes energy gets stuck and crying can help release it. I had to give myself permission to cry. Just cry, get it out.

Getting angry. Another way to sort out your solar plexus energy center is to allow yourself to get angry in a safe and controlled way. I go for a walk, way out in the desert so that I know no one can hear me and I scream and yell and cry and scream and yell and cry. Get it out. This also helps clear the throat chakra by expressing yourself. So your homework for this step is to next time you feel angry you find something (not someone) to punch or you go out and scream and yell, but the point is, get it out. Promise? I hope you do.

Energy work. To get your energy centers spinning effectively and clearly, see an energy worker. I went to an energy worker for eight years consistently and I have been one now, for many years. I can't even imagine what my life would be like without the help that I received. Just so you know it doesn't have to take years, or it could, depending on how much trauma you have to clear and heal. The point is to go as long as you want and need to. The outcome of this step is to add to your tool box ideas of how to help yourself and others when needed.

When you follow and implement these steps you will realize that there is more to the body than meets the eye. You will know and understand the seven energy centers. You will have the tools to clear your chakras and get them flowing freely.

Next we will explore healing.

If you'd like further support from me, please use this QR. Looking forward to hearing from you!

Chapter 11

HEALERS OF THE WORLD

What if "weird" worked? What if things that are weird, outside your comfort zone, or even outside your scope of understanding, still worked, still helped you?

Here I will explore healing modalities that can help you release pain/trauma.

Listen to your inner self and don't get pushed into doing something that doesn't feel right for you. I'll illustrate this in sharing a story of some of my therapy sessions.

You will also learn three steps to find the best modality for you:

1.   Research the different modalities.
2.   Choose the modality that you feel called to and trust that it will help.
3.   Go into the session with a clear intention and trust that it will help you.

Here, you'll understand that not all issues can be healed cognitively, there are many ways to get help with trapped trauma, to trust your intuition, to trust and receive the healing, and to know that you are in the right place at the right time!

Life is energy. And as such, it belongs to all, reaches all, and blesses all.

I was invited multiple times to participate in an ayahuasca ceremony. (Ayahuasca, a native hallucinogenic plant) I felt called to it. I had an open mind. It was a really special time, because I got to do it with my adult kids.

I had a beautiful experience. And I felt that it opened up my third eye, my spiritual sight. I was still really trying to make a difference in whatever way I could. But I was limited as to how much of a difference I could make because of my job. Ayahuasca started me on a new path. And so when I got out of sales, I started my healing center and started my coaching, and my migraines basically went away. I can't even remember the last time I had a migraine.

I had another really phenomenal experience with reiki, an energy healing technique. Marita, a beautiful soul, offered to do a session with me because I'd realized my heart chakra (spiritual power) was blocked. It was my first introduction to reiki. Marita worked on energetically removing it. As the session went on, I could tell that the blockage was getting smaller, I could totally see it in my mind's eye, I could feel it, and I knew when it was gone. Then I could feel the space that it had occupied, energetically.

We consciously filled that space with love and light. Since then, my relationships have become completely different, because I am now able to let people into my inner heart. I didn't even realize how much I was keeping people at arm's length. I just didn't trust them all the way in because I didn't want to get hurt again. I didn't want to feel the pain of betrayal or abandonment or rejection. Zander was right. So we removed that rock from my spiritual heart. I removed it with my intention to have it go, and she moved it with her ability to move energy.

When I had the opportunity to learn reiki, I took it. I knew I wanted to have that gift of being able to help people in the same way that Marita was able to help me. Now I'm a Reiki Master, and I'm able to help other people clear their energy centers/chakras and move energy. I'm thankful to have this tool in my toolbox.

Meditation is another amazing healing modality. I had an experience meditating, once, that I will never forget. I became nothing and everything all at once. I became one, I became one vibration. I became one with Source, with God, with everything, with the planet, with everybody, everything, all at once. Words don't work when you're trying to express an experience like that. When people used to say that we are one, at first I was like, "Yeah, we're one. Yes, we're all connected."

But when you have an experience like that, you truly get it. This 3-D dimension that we live in is not the same as the other dimensions that we can tap into. It's fun. It's fun to explore and see what all we can experience and find through meditation.

I realize that what I'm about to say is maybe going to blow some minds: time doesn't have to be linear. You've all heard the phrase, "Time is an illusion." Now I know why. It actually is. When you're in the fifth dimension, the space-time continuum is vertical. Everything that ever was or ever will be is all happening right now. I've had too many spiritual experiences, and I know too many people who have had such experiences, where time travel is experienced, in the present, when everything is happening now. I experienced this in a past-life-regression therapy session!

As a therapy, our healer was doing time regression with different individuals during different sessions. He did it with my sons, Brayden and Tate, and with different people, and realized that quite a few individuals were all going back to the same time. It was my turn.

I didn't yet know if I believed it or not. It didn't make any sense to me. How can you go back in time into other lifetimes? But it was an amazing journey, the likes of which I'd never before experienced. The boys didn't tell me anything, so that I wouldn't have any preconceived ideas. The healer took me aside and asked me what I saw. I wasn't sure at first. I thought I might have been doing it wrong. Then suddenly I saw everything, as if a movie were playing in my head.

The healer asked me what was next. I saw myself in Europe, with my emerald green embroidered dress, with my hair pulled back. I saw our house, a huge estate. My friend Gerry in real life was my husband in that vision. I could see his eyes, the bracelets he wore on his arms, the color of his shirt. I knew where our bedroom was, I could see it all. Prompted by the healer, I continued, saying we were walking to a secret meeting, without horses to avoid making noise. We arrived at a humble cottage. I was in the house now and saw my boys, I named other people I knew. "We're here for this meeting," I said, noting the intense energy and sense of purpose.

We were protecting a book and were discussing where to take it. The healer asked me to continue. I said we were going to hide the book in a false compartment on the floor of the carriage. The healer asked me to describe it. It was a big black, square carriage with wooden spoked wheels.

Then my boys showed up by "coincidence", not knowing I was doing a past-life-regression therapy. He called them in, and the three of us lay on mats on the floor. He led the boys back in time and over the next couple of hours we filled in different pieces of the story.

Josh knew we were all experiencing the same moments in time. Tate was married to a girl named Madison, whom we all loved very much. At the mention of the name Madison, I said, "that was my girl's name — in this lifetime, if I had a girl, that would've been her name." Now I know that this was Tate's wife in a past life.

In our past-life experiences, my boys were my brothers, not my sons. The healer asked what happened to Madison. I knew instantly. "She died in child-birth," I said. Tate, beside me, burst into tears. We all did, sobbing as if it had just happened.

We recovered from that after a while. I mentioned that Brayden was married to a blonde girl, adding quickly, "You had two kids." "A boy and a girl," he said. This was amazing. I could see Brayden with his son on his shoulders as they smiled at each other. The little girl was Sarah. I thought the boy's name was Robert, but it wasn't quite right. So I didn't say it. And then sure enough, Brayden beside me says "Yeah, I think my son's name was Robbie." And I'm like, "Yes, it was Robbie." Robert wasn't quite right. Robbie was the right name.

At this point, I was just in awe, I couldn't believe what was happening. In my recounting to the healer, we as a group moved this precious book into a large bookstore, so it could be hidden in plain sight. All of a sudden, I realized that I know that Brayden and his wife were murdered by the soldiers who were looking for the book. I didn't want to, but I knew I had to say it out loud. Brayden became angry and then so sad until he sobbed, and we all cried again. Then I realized something else, I said, "Gerry and I, took your kids, we took Robbie and Sarah and we raised them as if they were our own."

I realized at that moment, why I was so confident about taking in Zander when he was 16 (the troubled teen I had mentioned earlier in this book). People would question why I would be doing this, and I would simply know that I could. As a result of this session, I was aware that in a past life I had loved at least two other children as if they were mine.

After this experience, there is no doubt that I HAVE lived other lives and lifetimes. For me, there's just no other way. That experience was so real, it was so epic. All I know is that I am different after that. I see things differently. I understand now that I have things to heal in this lifetime, so that I don't have to repeat it again. I'm on a mission to learn, to seek, to understand, to heal, and to help others do the same. I love my life. I have never been so in love with my life, as right here, right now. I am doing exactly what I'm supposed to be doing. And it's a wonderful feeling. I'm right where I need to be. Healing is a wonderful thing.

Steps and Methods

Here is how you can learn from me:

1. Research the different modalities

To start, you could try **Sound Healing**. Sound Healing, also known as Sound Therapy, consists of the application of the voice and musical and vibratory instruments in the energy fields and on the physical body. Human beings have made use of sound since its creation to obtain and express information about the world around them, to communicate with each other, to heal, to transform, and, above all, to feel united. The vibration and sound work on our energy and auric body, balancing it through each of the chakras, and physically our bone structure, our spine, and every cell of our body to establish perfect harmony.

Here are some benefits of this therapy:

- It balances the physical, emotional, mental, and spiritual body.
- It eliminates muscle contractures.
- It helps to overcome psychological imbalances.
- It controls states of anxiety, depression, stress, insomnia and hyper-activity.
- It increases our energy, creativity, concentration, and capacity for action.
- It cleanses and energetically recharges our chakras.
- It facilitates meditation.
- It relieves headaches.
- It lifts moods.
- It raises the body's defenses.

Try Crystal Healing. Crystal healing is a holistic and natural therapy that taps into the energetic power of crystals and how they affect the body and mind. A crystal therapist will place healing crystals on or around a client to help unblock, focus, and direct energy.

Crystal healing is an energy-based system. This means it is based on the belief that we are all made up of different energies and that when this becomes stagnant, unbalanced or blocked, it can cause illness.

On an emotional and spiritual level, crystals can help enhance self-esteem, encourage clarity, and inspire a sense of peace and centeredness. I always have crystals on me or near me, depending on the reason I want them. I'm wearing my amethyst pendant right now as I write this because it helps me live with positive purpose. It helps me connect with Source.

Experience Reiki / Energy Work. One of the ways we can replenish our life force is by using Reiki.

Reiki is a holistic technique because it harmonizes and unblocks all planes of the human being, physical, mental, emotional, and spiritual. It does not attack the body in any way, and it does not create addiction or side effects, since no chemicals or elements foreign to the body are used, but only the life energy that is present in every living being.

Reiki can be used for:

- Releasing repressed emotions
- Increasing the energy level, providing physical and mental vitality
- Organic revitalization and rejuvenation of the whole organism; in most cases Reiki increases the effects of medical treatment when used in conjunction with it, never replacing it
- Reducing or eliminating anxiety
- Relieving suffering, whether physical, emotional, mental, or spiritual
- Helping to eliminate the daily stress we are subjected to by migraines, depression, menstrual cramps, constipation
- Helping to cleanse the body and mind of all types of toxins

Reiki really helped me open up my inner heart that I had been protecting for years. Healing my heart in this way has helped me in my relationships. I am so thankful for it!

Engage in Breath Work. Transformational breathing techniques can liberate old blockages, emotional baggage, and it heals and releases anxiety and depression, and it quiets mental chatter.

On a physical level, breath work alkalinizes your blood, supra oxygenates your organs and systems on a cellular level, and stimulates your *vagus nerve* (a cranial nerve; it regulates all internal organs), which is paramount in the body's healthy functioning.

Experiences with breath work vary from emotional release of old blockages and traumas, connection with spirit guides of the celestial dimensions, cellular full body orgasmic sensations, release of entities, and general peace and well-being.

Practice Meditation. Meditation is training in awareness. You're not trying to turn off your thoughts or feelings; you're learning to observe them without judgment. It's the ability to be present, to be fully engaged in the here and now.

I have had profound experiences in meditation, and I love so much the feeling of connection to the Source, the oneness, and love. I also know four people personally who have healed themselves of cancer using meditation. It is powerful.

You can read more about healing through meditation on my website in the blog section.

Consider Past-Life Regression. Past Life Regression is a gentle form of hypnotherapy that takes an individual back through time to their previous lives or incarnations by accessing memories and experiences that are normally hidden in their subconscious mind.

Past Life Regression can help you to reconnect with past life experiences, identify physical ailments, explore unresolved emotions, and acknowledge and embrace the key lessons learned through those lives.

My experience of past life regression transformed my life tremendously, and so I am in no way afraid to die. I know my soul has and will continue to live on.

Sample Plant Medicines (Ayahuasca/Bufo/Kambo/Mushrooms). One way is through a **Sacred Mushroom Ceremony**, using psilocybin.

Mother Earth gives us this powerful medicine for the healing of our soul, mind, emotions and heart. It works on so many levels to allow the practitioner, in a guided ceremony, to address, understand, and heal personal issues, no matter how deep or ancestral they may be. Furthermore, it cleans and activates your lower energy centers (chakras), allowing you to reconnect your roots to your great Mother that lovingly sustains all life.

Modern-day medicinal use of psilocybin is rapidly growing, to the point that it is currently being used to treat many ailments, such as PTSD, anxiety, panic attacks, depression, suicidal tendencies, Alzheimer's, dementia, and ADD, among many others.

It can be enjoyable, beautiful, colorful, loving, and healing experience that lasts approximately 4 to 5 hours. Highly recommended for anyone who is serious about transforming their lives.

Sample Kambo. Kambo is the use of an excretion from a frog in the Amazonian jungle. It is practiced as a healing technique, discovered first by the tribes there. It is practiced by both men and women, giving strength and endurance.

There are also neuropeptides in Kambo that circulate in the central nervous system that allow neurons to communicate with each other. The results of this are memory improvement, sleep improvement, more energy, mental clarity, among many other things. The wonderful thing is that the human body opens naturally to this substance, recognizing and accepting it, allowing for a unique, deep cellular cleaning.

Drink Ayahuasca. Ayahuasca is a brew made from the Banisteriopsis caapi and Psychotria viridis plants. Taking ayahuasca leads to an altered level of consciousness due to psychoactive substances in the ingredients. This drink was used for spiritual and religious purposes by ancient Amazonian tribes, still used as a sacred beverage by some religious communities in Brazil and North America, including the Santo Daime.

Ayahuasca is traditionally used for spiritual purposes for those who seek a way to open their minds, heal from past traumas, or simply experience an Ayahuasca Journey.

Many people who have taken Ayahuasca claim that the experience led them to positive, long-term, life-altering changes. Ayahuasca can help with depression, anxiety, mood disorders, PTSD, and more. Ayahuasca started me on my healing path. I will be forever thankful for it. My migraines are almost non-existent now, as well.

If called, you could try Sonoran Desert Toad (Bufo Alvarius). This is also known as "Sapito." This Mexican toad blesses mankind with a secretion "humanely" extracted from its parotid glands (containing bufotenine and 5Meo dmt) that is dried, methylated, and inhaled. It creates possibly the most transcendental and unique entheogenic and mystical experience known to man. It opens the bridge to our inner spiritual dimensions and gives us the opportunity to feel the fusion with our most ancestral memory of Oneness, with the Great Spirit of Our Creator and all of creation, thus eliminating the illusion of separation and reconnecting us with the greatest love and truth of all: that we are one.

This toad secretion has earned its name as the "God Molecule" for a good reason. The 15-minute indescribable journey is experienced on a cellular, molecular, and atomic level.

It is truly a life-changing experience, giving so much love into every fiber of your being that it has the potential to change paradigms and heal us of many ailments.

Try Rapé. Rapé is a mixture of healing plants and tobacco converted into powder that is gently blown into both nostrils. It is an Amazonian practice that has many therapeutic effects, with each tribe having their own unique preparations and blends.

Rapé has various physical healing properties, but on an energetic, emotional, and mental level it integrates and balances our masculine and feminine energies, calms internal mental chatter, and prepares the practitioner for a moment of clarity and relaxation, making it perfect for beginning a meditative practice or just a moment of clarity, connection, and contemplation with self.

Try Sananga. These natural eye drops are made from the root and bark of the Tabernaemontana Undulata tree and come from the kaxinawa tribes in the Brazilian amazon. This powerful, sacred medicine is used to clear energy blockages on an emotional, physical, and spiritual level. It can balance and increase your energy levels and has the potential to assist in locating the root cause of blockages and infirmities. It increases concentration, mental and spiritual focus, and clarity.

On a physical level, Sananga is known to improve or heal myopia, depth, and color perception difficulties, image definition, glaucoma, cataracts and even some cases of blindness.

There are many ways to get help with trapped trauma.

Step 2. Choose the modality that you feel called to, and trust that it will help.

Ask yourself, "Which modalities should I look into further?" Your answer could be from reading this list above, or maybe you have heard other people talking about one of them, and it piqued your interest, or you have felt a pull. Write down any that come to mind. And it's okay if nothing comes to mind.

Ask yourself, "Which modality should I follow?" If you've already written down some plant medicine, circle your answer. I started with Ayahuasca, but you should only do what you are called to do. If you don't receive an answer, that's your answer. Wait until you do.

Then research the plant medicine you feel directed to study. You will find both negative and positive things about anything you look up, just like almost anything in this online world we live in now.

The outcome of this step is to listen to your intuition and choose the modality you feel called to use.

Step 3. Go into a session with a clear intention and trust that it will help you.

If you decide to go ahead with a plant medicine ceremony, then once you confirm and set the date, the medicine already starts to work to prepare you. Know that you will probably get feelings of wanting to back out, of fear, etc. Know that this is normal and this is just your subconscious trying to protect you from something new and different. If you honestly feel that your higher self has led you to do it, then do it. If you think otherwise, then don't. I was nervous when I did ayahuasca, but I definitely felt led to do it. So I did.

The second step here is to go into the ceremony with confidence that it will be an experience that will help you, that it will be a benefit to you. Trust that you are in the capable loving hands of the universe, of Source. Visualize the smiles afterward and the amazing feelings you will feel as if they are happening now.

Have an intention of what you would like to see happen. Maybe it's a question answered, or maybe you want to rid yourself of anxiety, or some other ailment. Make sure you have a clear intention. You will use this throughout the ceremony.

When you follow and implement these steps, you will realize that there are healing modalities that may seem weird at first, but when called to use can transform your life. You will realize the importance of releasing pain/trauma. You have the three steps to find the best modality for you:

1. Research the different modalities.
2. Choose the modality that you feel called to and trust that it will help.
3. Go into the session with a clear intention for the session and trust it will help you.

These steps will help you know and understand that there are many ways to get help with trapped trauma. These steps will help you to trust your intuition and to trust and receive the healing — and to know that you are in the right place at the right time!

You can check out my Healing Center called Upaya. Which means "the art of navigating the illusion". The website is www.upayahealingcenter.com to learn more.

Two Ways to Live Your Life

There are only two ways to live your life: one is that nothing is a miracle. The other is that everything is a miracle. I choose the latter.

You can hone the healer in you, too! Everyone has a healer in them if they choose to activate it.

Here, I explore activating your healer, finding the best teacher, and putting in the time to learn well.

To illustrate this, I will show how one healer helped me.

Then you will be given three steps for becoming a healer yourself:

1. Identify what modality you feel called to work with.
2. Find a master of that modality and learn from them.
3. Practice, practice, practice!

I have had the amazing privilege of meeting a divine healer named Christian Mickelson. He is a friend and #1 Best-Selling Author of "Get Clients Today," and the creator of a notable sign-up system, "Free Sessions That Sell," a program designed specifically to help coaches, consultants, and healers easily sign up high-paying, high-end clients.

Christian is one of the best coaches on the planet, and he is also a healer. One day, we were having breakfast together with 10 people around the table. We were asking him questions about his Instant Miracle Healing, and he offered to help people in that moment, with whatever it was they were dealing with.

I watched him do his thing and then he turned to me and said, "Is there anything I can help you with?" I told him about my jumpy nervous system due to years of abuse and living in fear from my ex-husband, and that I had some tendinitis in my shoulder. So he started sending me energy using the Instant Miracle Technique. I literally twitched for probably seven minutes or more, right in the middle of the restaurant.

My ego wanted to say, "Don't do it, I must look weird." But I knew intuitively that I was getting help. So I surrendered. Then all of a sudden, it stopped. The results were that my shoulder hasn't given me trouble since, and my nervous system is tremendously better. People can walk up behind me now, and I don't jump out of my skin. It's amazing!

This had such an influence on me that I decided I needed to know how to do what he did. I wanted to be able to help people as he did, simply sitting around the breakfast table. I signed up and completed level one and level 2 and got certified in Instant Miracle, and it is a miracle. It's the only thing I can say. It's beyond what you can even imagine. I practice it constantly.

I had a friend come to visit when she was super depressed. I worked with her, and the depression went away. I worked on another individual whose shoulder was hurting for months. Several months later, he has not had any more shoulder issues. Just some of the conditions I've healed using this system are sexual abuse, traumatic experiences that people hold inside them, pain, dry mouth, anxiety, fear. I have never seen anything like it before in my life. I'm so thankful to have this tool in my toolbox to be able to help and serve.

If you'd like to know more about Instant Miracle, go to www.instantmiraclemastery.com

Steps and Methods

Here is how you can learn from my experiences:

Center yourself and work the Diamond of Freedom to get into a peak state.

Step 1. Identify what modality you feel called to work with.

To start, ask yourself, "Do I want to activate the healer in me?"

If you are already sure of this call, skip to Step 2. If you are not yet sure, hang with me a little bit longer for this discussion. I realized I wanted to activate the healer in me the moment I experienced healing from Christian using Instant Miracle.

Research different modalities you might wish to work with. This will take as long as it takes to research the modalities that interest you.

Ask yourself, "Which modality should I focus on and learn first?"

Choose the one you are most excited about and called to. The others can come later, just like with me. I learned reiki first, then sound and crystal healing, then Kambo, and then Instant Miracle. It takes time to practice and master a modality, so taking them one at a time is advised. So, get started!

Step 2. Find a master of that modality and learn from them.

Research a few different Masters of your modality to make sure they have years of experience. If you can find one via a referral, that is always helpful. That is how I have found all of my Master Teachers — by referral.

Ask yourself, "Is this my Master Teacher or not?"

Make sure they are aligned with the value of loving and serving. There is a lot of spiritual ego, even in this arena. Take a minute to slow down and feel and listen to how you feel around them. Listen to your answer — Trust it!

Hire the one you feel you can best learn from. It's important that there be an exchange of energy in that you pay them money or some other kind of trade. If they train you for free, things will end up unbalanced, so make sure there is an exchange of energy of some sort.

Get started as soon as you can. Don't delay.

If you are led to learn it, then start learning it right away.

Step 3. Practice, practice, practice!

Put time in with your teacher. Step one here is to put in the time with your Master Teacher. It will take time and energy to learn something new. Make sure when you start learning a healing modality that you have the proper time allocated to learn it and to learn it well. Immerse yourself. Get in as much time as you can. The world needs you.

Practice, practice, practice. You just have to do it. At first it will be a little weird and nerve-wracking, but that's life. Anytime you do something new, you get those feelings. So practice anyway.

Make sure that when you are "finished" with your teacher that you schedule times to revisit with them to review and uplevel yourself even more. There is always more to learn; you never completely arrive. When you learn from a Master Teacher, immersion and spaced repetition is how you truly master anything.

When you follow and implement these steps, you will be able to start the process of honing the healer in you, too! You will know how to find the best teacher and the importance of putting in the time to learn it well. You have the three steps on how to activate and become a healer yourself. They are:

1. Identify what modality you feel called to work with.
2. Find a master of that modality and learn from them.
3. Practice, practice, practice!

This step helps you get started in finding and hiring a Master to teach you, and you'll learn that practice makes perfect! You will learn the steps to take, if you want to learn a specific modality of healing, or how to master anything, for that matter.

In our next chapter, we will explore the power of love.

 If you'd like further support from me, please use this QR. Looking forward to hearing from you!

Chapter 12

LOVE IS THE ANSWER

We've been told a lot of lies about love. In this chapter, you'll find out how to untangle everything that you've been told or learned about love, so that you can love as you wish to love and be loved, unconditionally.

If you don't make a change, more shit will come, as you'll see in a story about ending my abusive marriage to my husband Joe. I will share three steps on how to figure out how the lies about love have affected you and how to make a change:

1. The lies we have been told about love
2. The cost of bullshit
3. The consequences of buying into the bullshit

You will learn the fallacy and fantasy of what we have been taught about love. You will discover the cost of continuing to believe the lies. It is now time to make your choice as to what you will continue to believe.

Many of us in the world are caught up in lies about love.

Sometimes, to know what love is, we have to know what love isn't. I've been through a lot to learn what love isn't. I grew up in a loving home with my immediate family, but things changed when I married Joe. I knew what love was, but I didn't experience that with Joe — at least, not from the day of our wedding on. Joe abused and used the Bible to his benefit, as many do, and he took it to an extreme.

My experience with Joe taught me that love is jealous, love is controlling, and love is sex. Fortunately, I later learned that these ideas about love are simply not true.

The Truth about Love

I arranged to meet Joe at a McDonald's to tell him that I was no longer going back to him, that we were done. I was nervous about what he would do. So I made sure that it was in a public place, and a plainclothes policeman was nearby, in case things got bad. We sat across from each other for the first time in a year. I told him it was over. He looked at me with anger and said, "Why? I brought you a soda once."

I sat there stunned. I couldn't help but laugh at the absurdity. "You brought me a soda once! What? You think by bringing me a soda once, that that's enough to sustain a relationship. That's why we're done."

As I looked back on our married relationship, he was right. He had brought me a soda once. I vaguely remember him handing me a Twizzlers once as well. But other than that, he had given me a soda once in eight years of marriage. I realize that this sounds crazy. How could it be true? But it is true.

This is what love isn't. With Joe, I experienced the extreme side of what love isn't. And yet I stayed for eight years, because I believed things that weren't true. For instance, I believed the lie that life is hard. I believed that I had to submit because I was the woman and he was the man, that I had to give him my body whenever he wanted it, that I had to stay married. And I believed that there was no way out without God being very displeased with me. It was even suggested that bad things could happen to me, or my children could die, if I displeased God.

We women have been lied to. Life is hard, but it doesn't have to be *that* hard!

My life is not perfect, but it is glorious, because of all the tools I've obtained and the different ways that I now look at things because someone taught me, and because I live them out in my life.

I now know the difference between fake and real love, and I know the contrast.

So I am thankful for my experience with Joe. He was my Master Teacher because thanks to him I know what love is not. And that is a gift. I know what control is. I can see it a mile off. I know what jealousy is. I know the difference between sex for sex, and sex in love. Completely different. I'm so thankful to know the difference.

Steps and Methods

Here is how you can learn from my experience.

Center yourself and work the Diamond of Freedom. Ask Source in you and all around you for wisdom, truth and clarity as you answer the next questions.

Step 1. Discover the lies we have been told about love

The first lie we have been told from our society, school, TV, and the media as a whole is that "sex is love."

We see it over and over. Victims of crime tell us that one in five girls and one in twenty boys is a victim of child sexual abuse. Self-report studies show that 20% of adult females and 5% to 10% of adult males recall a childhood sexual assault or sexual abuse incident.

Many of my clients, when expressing their story about their being sexually abused, tell me that they are told their abuser was just showing them love. Joe believed that the Bible told him he could do what he pleased with my body. It's a lie. We can see that bright and clear when it comes to sexual abuse, but can we see it in the more subtle programming that we receive?

Ask yourself, "Where do I believe, or where have I believed, this lie that, sex is love, or love is sex?"

Is it in how you carry yourself, is it in how you dress, is it in how you relate to your sexual partner? Write down anything that comes to mind without judgment.

"Love is control." This is the second lie.

So many people are controlled in the name of love. I can't even tell you how many of my clients have mentioned this in regards to their spouses, parents, churches, and especially their belief in how God feels about them based on their specific religion. Grown adults are scared to live their own lives because of how their loved ones or church parishioners will react if they go against what is wanted or expected. It's a lie.

Control is not love — it's simply control. Controlling someone for the most part is self-serving. Parents do it to their kids on a level that makes me ill. I did it, too, in the early days before I was taught not to.

When we control someone, we fill the need for significance ("I'm in control") and also the need for certainty ("I know what is going to happen because I'm in control"). Control also serves the need of love and connection ("I love you so much, that's why I'm not going to let you screw up your life").

Bullshit. Control is not love — control is nothing but control.

Ask yourself, "Where have I been controlled or been controlling under the guise of love?"

Write down whatever comes to mind, without judgment.

"Love is jealous." This is the third big lie we are told about love.

Jealousy is one of the ickiest things to experience. I've seen it over and over again with different clients and friends. It's this belief that if a significant other is jealous, they are an asshole, but if they aren't jealous, then they don't actually love you. What? That mental programming is just crazy, and yet I see it over and over again. I've watched both sides behave in ways to make the other person jealous, then when they are, it's a problem. This is not love.

Jealousy is not love — it's just jealousy.

Ask yourself, "Where have I believed the lie that jealousy is love?"

Write down anything that comes to mind, without judgment.

This step helps you weed out the various sorts of bullshit we are told about love.

Step 2. The cost of believing the bullshit.

Ask yourself, "Which lie has hurt me the most?"

Read over your list of lies about love that you either believe or used to believe. Circle the answer that's true for you.

Ask yourself, "How has this affected my life?"

Write down your answer, without judgment. I wasn't able to be guided by Source in me. Rather, I was controlled, instead, by the men in my life.

Ask yourself, "Who else's life has this affected, and how?"

For me, all that bullshit affected my kids the most. I didn't leave my marriage for years past when I could have and should have. My kids and I went through years of abuse because I believed the lie that he had the right to control me and use me sexually and that all of it was love. And I believed that I needed to control my kids' every move because that's what a loving parent does. It's a lie.

This step can help you see and feel the cost of believing the lies we're told about love.

Step 3. What are the consequences if we continue to buy this bullshit?

Ask yourself, "If I keep believing these lies what will the consequences likely be?"

This is an important question. Play out the answers in all their horrid detail for a minute or two. Write everything down.

Ask yourself, "How much pain and suffering will I experience if I continue with these beliefs?"

Write down everything that comes to mind. I know that If I had continued to believe that sex, control, and jealousy were love, I would have stayed in that abusive, loveless marriage. I wouldn't know what true freedom is, I wouldn't know what true love is. I wouldn't know what it felt like to be led by my inner higher self.

Ask yourself, "Whose life will I affect if I keep this up?"

Write down who comes to mind, without judgment. My kids would have grown up to believe the same thing, and they would likely treat the people around them in the same ugly way. There are always consequences to our beliefs.

Choose. Choose whether you wish to continue to believe the lie and live out the lie, or not. It is your choice, no one but yours.

This step helps you predict what you and others' future will be like if you don't make a change.

When you follow and implement these steps, you will understand the importance of realizing that we have been lied to about love. You will know clearly how it has impacted you, and you will know that, if you don't make a change, more shit is coming. You have the three steps for figuring out how the lies about love have affected you and how to make a change. They are:

- Learn what lies we have been told about love.
- Learn about the cost of bullshit.
- Learn about the consequences if you continue to buy the lies.

Here you've learned the fallacy and fantasy of what we have been taught that love is, and how those beliefs have shaped your life so far, and how they will affect your future.

Understand that You Didn't Understand

Love is messy. Here, I'm exploring the importance of owning your own shit, of forgiving yourself and whoever hurt you.

To illustrate this, I will share my story of what I've done in this regard,

Then you will learn steps to move on from old relationships and to create new ones:

1. Forgive yourself.
2. Forgive them.
3. Attract true love.

Raise your frequency as high as you possibly can, consistently as you can, and you will attract someone of like frequency.

You will learn that often we have to learn the hard way. You'll know how important it is to look back and evaluate what you've learned. You'll know that working on ourselves creates life-changing magic.

I didn't have the best experience of what love is in a marriage, in a male-female relationship. I can see now how that affected the relationships that followed.

I understand now that I didn't understand true love at the time. It got messy at times. And I stayed longer with some of the people I had dated than I probably should have, just because I didn't want to quit, and I wanted to be loved. I wanted to have that deeply personal connection every day, however I could get it.

I didn't understand what a true loving relationship looked like.

I forgive myself and them for these times and for these relationships, because I realized that we both didn't understand. We were two people who didn't understand love, trying to make it work.

Steps and Methods

Here is how you can learn from my experience.

Center yourself and work the Diamond of Freedom if necessary.

Step 1. Forgive yourself

To start, ask yourself, "Where in the matters of love have I brought someone pain?"

Write down what comes to mind, without judgment. I wrote down that I unintentionally brought my dating partners pain by staying longer than was healthy or kind to both of us.

Ask yourself, "What specifically did I do, and how did it impact them?"

Write down what comes to mind.

Then apologize. Own your mistakes.

Apologize to those you have hurt knowingly or unknowingly. You can have an understanding that you did not clearly understand love, or else you wouldn't have acted that way. It is amazingly healing to apologize to whomever you have hurt and to go one step further, and ask them how your actions impacted them. There may be more pain to uncover there. If there is, own it, apologize. Even if they don't own their mistakes, own yours. You will be amazed at how healing it can be for you and for them.

The outcome of this step is take responsibility for how your actions affected your past relationships.

Step 2. Forgive them.

Ask yourself, "Who in my life do I feel has wronged me in some way, and it still upsets me?"

Listen to your inner voice and write down anything that comes to mind.

For example, I was very upset for years over how Joe treated the boys and me. It was abusive, even dangerous. I felt at times that he wanted to kill me or all of us.

Ask yourself, "What was my part in it, and what else could have caused them to act the way they did?"

In other words, change your perspective. Go outside of the program and think differently. I realized that Joe grew up in a very difficult environment. He was not taught nor did he experience unconditional love. So I realize now that he did not understand how to truly love.

Release them. Forgive, understand, but let the situation — let the pain — go.

This step is intended to help you get closure — and to be free!

Step 3. Attract True Love.

Raise your frequency as high as you possibly can. The first step in owning your mistakes and turning things around is to raise your frequency as high as you possibly can by working the Diamond.

As I've noted before, the Diamond is a four-step process of getting your shit together and changing your state of being. The first step is to change the position of your body by smiling, breathing, and moving it.

The second point is to change what you are focused on, and ask yourself, "What am I thankful for?"

The third step is to replace the bullshit you are telling yourself, as in this instance, "Poor me, I'm a victim, so and so did X to me," and change it to, "I'm fine, because everyone does stupid/ hurtful things sometimes, including me, as we are all learning and growing."

And the fourth point of the Diamond is to connect to Source and know you are not alone and ask for divine help.

Change your frequency, change your life. Work that Diamond over and over until you feel love and gratitude. Do it now, please.

Work the Diamond consistently. This is not a "one and done" thing. I am continuously working on the Diamond.

Repeat a mantra that serves you by reminding yourself, "I have all the love I need inside me now." Feel free to copy this one.

When it comes to matters of the heart, this is the best mantra for me: Magic can happen when we work on ourselves and raise our frequency.

When you follow and implement these steps, you will realize that love is messy, and it's important to own your mistakes. It's important to forgive yourself and whoever hurt you. You will also have a new mantra that inspires you, like mine: "All the love I need is within me now."

You have steps to move on from old relationships and how to create the one you want:

1. Forgive yourself.
2. Forgive them.
3. Attract true love — change your frequency, change your life.

The outcome is to learn how to raise your frequency as high as you possibly can, consistently as you can, and you will attract someone of like frequency. Realize that when we work on ourselves and raise our frequency, magic happens.

True Love Is Like Ghosts

Do you believe in ghosts? Many people talk about them, but few have actually seen them. That's what true love is like.

Do you know what love is? Do you know what's possible?

Here I'm exploring the emotions and actions of love. I will share the story of the love that I have with my partner now and how we navigate life together.

You will also learn three steps on what love is:

1. What is true love?
2. What does love look like, act like — how does it feel?
3. BE LOVE. Keep believing!

With this step, you can come to a relationship with a full cup and to just be love, be loving, do whatever is the most loving thing in every situation. You will learn what love is actually, what unconditional human love is capable of.

So what is real love? What is actually possible?

Over the years, I have progressively chosen better partners. The relationship I am in now is the most amazing relationship I've ever had, and that I knew in my heart of hearts was possible. I feel so blessed, I feel like the luckiest girl on the planet to have this man by my side. He's not ahead of me, he's not behind me — we're partners. Actual partners. And it's a beautiful thing. So what is love? What is actual love?

First things first: You have to love yourself. If you don't love yourself, you don't have love to give. Love yourself for all you are and for all you are not. I had things I didn't love about myself, but eventually I learned to love myself and to look at what I considered my physical or emotional flaws to be gloriously human. Permission to be human is an amazing thing! So learn to love yourself for all you are and for all you are not.

In a healthy relationship, you have to come from a full cup already. And everything else is an overflow. But if you come with a half cup expecting that other person to fill it — ding, ding, ding. Sirens should be going off. No, this is not love. This is taking. Love is loving them just the way they are, and just the way they're not. Let me say that again: love is loving them just the way they are, and just the way they're not. In other words, you're not trying to change them.

Love is them loving you, just the way you are, and just the way you're not. I had never heard that before until I met the incredible man that I'm with right now. He looked me in the eyes and said, "I love you just the way you are and just the way you're not." In that moment I felt complete freedom. I thought my heart would burst, would explode! Complete freedom to just be me in all the things that I am, and all the ways that I'm not.

Here are some things to look at when you're considering a partner. It's important for you to be aligned emotionally, physically, economically, and spiritually with them. Emotionally, my partner and I have both had massive amounts of training and coaching. We are able to separate ourselves from the program. We can look at things and see our triggers and separate ourselves from them, and say, "Oh, interesting. Something just happened there. What's going on?"

And we're usually able to not take it personally and just look at it and go, "Oh, yeah, I am triggered. Hmm, I wonder why? Maybe it's this past situation that is creeping into my present." And we're able to annihilate those old beliefs and patterns.

Economics are important, too. I've been in different relationships where the economic difference was massive, and it can really be hard. I'm not saying it's impossible, but it can really be challenging. If one person is in a significantly different position economically, it can make things super tricky due to the running program in our society that say the one with the money has the power and control. Be aware.

Being aligned spiritually is important as well. We have slightly different beliefs. But ultimately, we know there's a higher power, and we love living our lives listening and seeking to understand just how big the Divine/Source/ God is.

Love means your heart feels like soaring. That's what love does. Love is two people going all in. Not halfway, but all in, playing full out. And what does playing full out look like? It means you're looking at how you can make their day better. And when both lovers are doing that, not just one side —I've been on that train, and it's not so fun—but when both lovers are seeking to serve each other and seeking to bring joy to each other, then — Wow! That's like a rocketship to heaven!

Love is when each person takes 100% responsibility for their shit, and there IS shit. We need to stop being surprised that there's shit to deal with. But when each person takes responsibility for their shit, that's love. Not making the other person responsible: "My shit, my responsibility. Let me clean that up, and I am sorry."

Love is, your needs are my needs. When both partners do this—BOOM! Fireworks!

Love is freedom. You are free to be you, because you and they love everything you are and everything you're not. And they are free to be them because you love everything that they are and everything they're not. I want to make clear that this doesn't mean that abuse is okay, or that you need to accept that. You can love them, but you might need to let them go.

This love that I'm experiencing now is glorious. I now know what real love is in a healthy, romantic relationship. I am so thankful to know what love isn't, and now to know what love truly is.

Love is epic. I encourage us all to.... "Be Love."

Be that next loving thing. Have so much love in your own heart that it's full and overflowing. You have all the love that you need inside you, right here, right now. Be Love. I went online and designed a hat that says, "Be Love" on it. I wear it a lot as a reminder for myself and hopefully to others to, Be Love.

Love really is the answer. If you're going to be something, Be Love.

Steps and Methods

Here is how to learn from my experience.

Step 1. What is true love?

To start, love yourself just the way you are. Think of something right now that you dislike about yourself. Write it down. Think about the thing that you chose about yourself, and see if you can't find a blessing or benefit in it. This doesn't mean you don't continue to learn and grow. You can always learn to be examples of more love and grace.

Love others just the way they are. What is something that your significant other, or roommate, or friend does that normally makes you crazy?

Write it down. Now see if you can find the blessing or gift in that thing. This changes everything. You will look at everyone differently, because if you can see your partner differently and accept their humanness, then you can also accept others who make human mistakes.
You will know you are truly loved when others love you just the way you are. It starts with you loving yourself for just the way you are and just the way you are not.

This step will help you know what love truly is!

Step 2. What does it look like, act like? How does it feel?

Practice alignment.

In a healthy partnership, four things need to be in alignment:

Emotionally
Physically
Economically
Spiritually

If any of these things are out of alignment in a big way, it can be difficult to sustain the relationship. So ask yourself, "Where am I not in alignment with my partner?"

Write down your answer. Make time to talk with them about it to see if you can find a way to be more aligned.

Love makes your heart sing. Are we lighting up when our partner enters the room? If not, your love needs some time and attention. Love is an action. It's not passive. If you treat it passively, it will die.

Be all-in, 100%.

The next step in creating a healthy loving relationship is to understand that it's not a 50/50 thing. It requires 100% and 100%, each person giving it all they have. Otherwise, it creates a situation where both people are trying to take what they need from the other. This is not love. Are you putting 100% into your relationship? If not, change that, acknowledge it with your partner, go all in and watch the magic happen. You move first, you shift first. Make their needs your needs.

Love allows you the freedom to be you. When you truly love someone, you don't possess them. The secret is to let them be free to be, and when they are doing the same for you — magic! Do you allow your partner the freedom to be themselves? Do they allow you to be yourself?

Each person takes 100% responsibility. Own your shit. When you get selfish, unkind, or forget how to truly love, take responsibility. Say sorry, ask how it impacted them (don't assume you know), listen, and don't defend. When both people do this, it truly is epic.

Respect each other.

If you don't, it won't last, or if it does last, it won't be happy. Respect your partner for all that they are. Appreciate what it took for them to be who they are. See the good, see the amazing, focus on those things.

Are you respecting your partner? Write down your answer. Write down a list of things you respect about your partner, friend, or child.

Serve each other. Love is service. Notice I didn't say selfishness. Love is to be happy in your service to the person you love.

Think about the love a mom has for their child. I know there are some of you who did not have a loving parent, but hopefully you were able to create that for yourself as a mother or father yourself. Are you serving the people you love? Are they serving you? This is something important to look at and pay attention to. Remember, be the first to serve, to change, to shift.

Last but not least, seek to bring joy to each other. Get creative on how you can do that. Are you thinking about ways to bring them joy? If you aren't, then ask yourself, "What could I do to bring a massive smile to my partner's face?" Listen. Then do it.

The outcome of this step is to have a new idea of what love actually is.

Step 3. BE LOVE. Keep believing.

Love yourself just the way you are. Remember that you have all the love you need inside you now. Love without conditions.

Be an example of love in your actions. Live this unconditional love out in your life and in your actions. Be the living, breathing example of love.

When you follow and implement these steps, you will know what love is and what is possible, that real love does exist, and the importance of understanding the emotions and actions of love. You will know that it is your responsibility to come from a full cup, that everything else is an overflow. To recap:

What is true love?
What does it look like, act like?
How does it feel?
BE LOVE. And keep believing in love.

This step should help you know what love is! To come to a relationship with a full cup and to Be love, be loving, do whatever is the most loving thing in every situation. You will learn what love is and what unconditional human love is capable of.

Universal Love

The novelist Alexander McCall Smith has written, "Love is the discovery of ourselves in others, and the delight in the recognition."

I love that so much, and that's what we're exploring here: my pursuit of love and my realization of what true love is. I'll share an experience from my family and my woman's group, and then you'll get steps to understanding universal love:

We are all one.
We are all droplets of god.
Love is Divine, and Divine Love is the answer to all problems.

From this exercise, you can have a more sure sense of what love can be, and you can feel and be loved everywhere.

I get to experience this in my life with an amazing women's group that I'm part of. There are usually 10 to 15 of us, and we get together weekly. The oneness that we get to experience together, the unconditional love that we express on a daily basis on a chat that we share, and then weekly via Zoom, is like nothing I've ever experienced.

I didn't know that people could actually be unconditionally loving, consistently loving, other than my family. I didn't know that it was possible. I've met so many people lately who are all about love. We are all energy, and therefore we are all connected.
So: Be Love.

Steps and Methods

Here is how you can move forward with this:

Step 1. We are one.

"If you want to find the secrets of the universe, think in terms of energy, frequency, and vibration," said Nikola Tesla. We are all energy, and therefore we are all connected. I have experienced this many times when doing long-distance energy healing. People can be thousands of miles away from me, but I can feel them and they can feel me. We are all connected.

Ask yourself, "Where in my life do I know it to be true that we are all connected?" Listen, and write down your answers.

If we are all connected, totally connected, then I am you and you are me. This is how we can feel the feelings of others. We are more the same than we are different, but people innately see others as separate from themselves and focus on the ways in which they are separate.

But a dramatic part of the human experience is being with another person, and suddenly realizing the ways in which they are similar to oneself. After having an experience like this, people begin to realize that what is inside of one person is the same as what's inside of another person. They begin to realize that which is within themselves and that which is within others is indeed One, and that there truly is no "other."

Ask yourself, "Where in my life have I experienced that I am you and you are me?"

Listen, and write down what comes to mind. I feel this in my women's group. It's a wonderful thing to share this human experience with other humans.

Ask yourself, "Where have I experienced the understanding that if I hurt you, I hurt me?" Listen, and write down your answers.

The hope here is that you will understand that we are one, and that we are not alone. We are all in this together.

Step 2. We Are All Droplets of God

The importance of this is to realize that we are all made of God — not the same quantity, but the same quality.

God is the whole, the body of water. We are drops from that body of water. We are parts of the whole. We are not the same quantity, but we have the same quality. Gather all the droplets back together, and we are one.

Ask yourself, "Do I know in my heart that this is true?" Write down your answer.

If this is true for you, as it is for me, this means we can take advantage and enjoy more strength, more intelligence, more intuition, more power, more than we have even been taught to believe. We are one with God, we have God in us, for real.

Take a minute to let this soak in. I had all kinds of limits on myself until I really accepted this to be fact. I didn't believe that the God in me could help heal people, until I did believe, and now Source in me, and I as the conduit, do.

There is no space between the parts. We just think there is. We create separation. This is the biggest secret of the universe. We are One.

Accept that we are parts of God.

3. God/ Universe/ Source/ The Divine Is Love and Love Is the Answer

God is One because he is the Source of everything. There is nothing other than God.

I do this step by sharing the story of living out love everyday with the people, animals, and nature that exists around me.

People forget that God is love, and they make things conditional. This is not God's way.

God's Love is unconditional.

We don't have to do anything or believe anything to gain favor. We are already in favor and will always BE IN FAVOR with God. We are unconditionally loved. Period.

Take a reflective moment to fully absorb that!

You are unconditionally loved by The Universe, by Source, by God. God is in you, and so you have all the love you need inside you. You, also, can love unconditionally. Period.

Repeat after me: "I am Love."

Breathe again: "I am Love."

You are Love. God is Love. We are all connected. We all are Love.

Love is the answer.

Period.

 If you'd like further support from me, please use this QR. Looking forward to hearing from you!

CONCLUSION

Our journey has only begun. We should all best appreciate the wonder of life as we experience it. There are many paths of glory to discover!

In this book, I have taken you on my journey. I've shared with you some details of my childhood, my life with the Mission, my work as a missionary, my abusive marriage, the thrills and challenges of motherhood, the joy of self-discovery, my life in Mexico, and my passion for service and for helping others. Thank you for sharing my challenges and for embracing my methods to uncover your own inner truths and guidance!

You have received several series of steps, methods, and suggestions to help you dig deep within yourself, to center yourself, and to move forward toward becoming the happy, free person you want to be.

You should have the tools now, and the encouragement, to create new belief systems for yourself to help you move out of your childhood traumatic experiences, or lingering fears brought on by things you've experienced in life as a child or as an adult.

You can create new ways of approaching life, of reaching out to others, of changing your perspective — and of living a happy, healthy, productive, and extraordinary life.

You now know how to go from Fear to Freedom!

Let's all celebrate!!!

Amy Joy

is a #1 International Best Selling Author, a Breakthrough Strategist at Amy Joy Coaching and is founder and CEO of Upaya Healing Center.

She has been the Top Sales Representative for PROVAC for many years as well as an Assistant Manager, leading by example on how to influence and sell ethically.

Amy is also currently a proud coach for Wingman Coaching, a sacred Kambo facilitator, Reiki master, and is certified in Sound, Instant Miracle, and Crystal Healing.

Amy worked 4 years as a missionary in the jungles of Papua New Guinea, is a single mother of two sons by birth plus another son by unofficial adoption. She escaped an abusive marriage, started over in a foreign country and is now thriving and living her best life.
She is also a child of the planet, having visited 62 countries.

Amy loves people and is passionate about helping and inspiring them to live extraordinary lives.